THE STREETS LIED
AND WE BELIEVED

DAVON MCNEIL

Published By

Freebird Publishers
Post Office Box 541
North Dighton, MA 02764
info@freebirdpublishers.com
www.FreebirdPublishers.com

Copyright © 2016 by Davon McNeil

All rights reserved. No part of this book may be reproduced in any form or by any means without the prior written consent of the Publisher, except in brief quotes used in reviews.

All rights reserved.

ISBN: 978-1541183643
ISBN-13: 1541183649

DEDICATION

This book is dedicated to my Grandma and Grandpa (RIP), and to my two beautiful daughters, Shalese and Juel McNeil

ACKNOWLEDGMENTS

To the Black Queen who gave birth to me!

Ma, I love you with all my heart. To this very day, I still wonder how you managed to raise three boys on your very own. You gave us everything we ever wanted and all of what we needed (smile). I want to apologize for all the pain I caused you and for all the days you had to take off from work to come support me at my many court arraignments. I also want to apologize for the numerous times the police came to the house looking for me, causing you embarrassment.

I'm sorry, Ma. You're the true love of my life. You raised me the best way you knew how and bestowed upon me your purest love. You did everything you were supposed to do as a mother. But it was mathematically impossible and against the law of nature for you to teach me how to become a man, but you sure did try your best with those a@#whoopings (smile). When I finally left home to run them streetz, I had no idea of all the heartache, chaos, destruction and iniquity I would cause you, myself, other families, my community and all the people who truly love me. You always told me that I wouldn't appreciate your wisdom (wise words) until was forced to. As I sit in this lonely 8xl0 cell, I can honestly admit that you were absolutely right. I love you, Ma!

To my enlightener, Allah Fu-Quan

Lord, you blessed me with the greatest gift in existence which is Knowledge of Self. This book would have never been born into matter if not for your wisdom (wise words) being the piece with magnetic and attracting I-Self. You got in the mud with me, God. And you introduced me to a Culture (way of life) that allowed 1-7 to transcend the (6). Eye'm forever grateful, Sun of Man. I love U-Allah.

To all the True & Living Gods who added on to this Cipher, I thank you. To the glorious Nation of Gods & Earths, I sincerely love Allah's (Our Fathers) world. The babies are the greatest!

To my NOI (Nation of Islam) brothers and my Sunni Muslim Brothers, I love and respect you all. Let's continue doing our job of enlightening our people, regardless to whom or what.

To all my comrades whom I met along this journey; stay strong and focused. Please keep your heaven (MIND) protected at all times! Peace is the way of the righteous.

To all of those who stayed true, I sincerely thank you. There are too many to name, but you know who you are. I love you all. I was able to get through this struggle because of your continued and unwavering support.

To my family - I love all of you supremely! We're way too deep to name us all, so I won't even attempt it. We've had to struggle our entire lives and we've all experienced our share of hardships. But through it all, our love has remained extremely unbreakable. We're the nation of forever people!

Dad, I love you. I could never be mad at you for your absence because that would be hypocritical of me. But I did go through hell in them streetz without your guidance. You've been one of my main supporters during my incarceration and I truly honor you for that. I challenge you to be there for all the ones behind me. I love you, Old Head (smile).

By Davon McNeil

TABLE OF CONTENTS

DEDICATION _____ *i*

*ACKNOWLEDGMENTS*_____ *i*

*TABLE OF CONTENTS*_____ *iv*

AUTHOR'S NOTES _____ *viii*

THE STRUGGLE _____ *1*

COME RIDE WITH ME _____ *4*

*AGELESS*_____ *6*

THE NATURAL ORATOR _____ *8*

LIFE IS THE REVEALER _____ *10*

OF TRUTH _____ *10*

YOU'LL NEVER KNOW UNTIL YOU'VE BEEN THERE __ *13*

LIFE OF A LIFER _____ *15*

FAMOUS QUOTES _____ *16*

*REAL WISDOM FOR*_____ *19*

THE STREETS _____ *19*

*NO EXPLANATION*_____ *22*

*TO THE YOUNG QUEEN*_____ *24*

LIVE FROM THE AVE _____ *26*

*THE LIE*_____ *28*

SELF _____ *29*

FATHERLESS SON'S _____ *30*

CELL TIME _____ *32*

SOLO IS MY MOVEMENT _____ *34*

CHECKMATE, YOUR MOVE _____ *36*

AS SALAM WALAIKUM _____ *39*

LIVE _____ *40*

AUR-NUR: THE LIGHT _____ *42*

QUIET STORM _____ *45*

CARRY YOUR CROSS _____ *47*

TRIALS AND TRIBULATIONS _____ *49*

I'M SORRY LITTLE LADY _____ *51*

DAMN YOU PRISON _____ *54*

LOST AND NOW FOUND _____ *58*

YOUNG QUEEN, YOU'RE DIVINELY BLESSED _____ *61*

FRONTLINE SOULJA _____ *62*

ECONOMICS _____ *64*

L.I.F.E. _____ *67*

WHEN YOU'VE GOT _____ *71*

A GOOD WOMAN _____ *71*

TREAT HER RIGHT _____ *71*

SHE IS SO DAMN FILTHY _____ *73*

SCRIPTURE	*77*
THIS IS HOW I SEE IT	*80*
THE BARS WERE MADE TO HOLD Y'ALL...	*82*
ME AGAINST YOU	*85*
FOOD FOR THOUGHT	*88*
IN THE NAME OF ALLAH AND JUSTICE	*91*
MY YOUTH GONE!	*93*
WE WILL MAKE IT	*96*
REMEMBERING THE PAST	*99*
WHY ARE YOU SO MAD?	*100*
WE'VE BEEN LIED TO	*101*
LIVE A LIFE THAT MATTERS	*104*
EVERYTHING!!!	*106*
THE COMMUNITY OF BROTHERS	*108*
THE SECRET TEACHING THAT CHANGED RAP	*110*
THE GAME	*118*
THROUGH THE FIRE	*120*
I FOUND IT...PEACE	*122*
HUMANITY IS YOUR TRUE SELF	*125*
THE SCIENCE TO INCREASE KNOWLEDGE	*126*
PEACE, YOUNG QUEEN	*128*
WHY?	*129*

MY PHILOSOPHY _____ *130*

I LOVE YOU, DADDY _____ *133*

MY VISION _____ *135*

MY PAIN RUNS DEEP _____ *137*

MRS. STREETZ! _____ *140*

I DON'T OWE THE STREETZ NOTHIN'! ____ *142*

BROKEN SPIRITS _____ *145*

DAVON, PLEASE UNDERSTAND _____ *147*

PEACE AND BLESSINGS _____ *150*

WE CAME TO SEE YOU, BUT WE COULDN'T GET IN... *151*

IT WAS COLD OUT THERE _____ *153*

MY FIRST BORN CHILD _____ *155*

PAIN IN MY HEART _____ *157*

CHOICES _____ *160*

I REMEMBER _____ *162*

IT'S NOT A GAME AT ALL _____ *164*

CONCLUSION _____ *166*

ABOUT THE AUTHOR _____ *169*

AUTHOR'S NOTES

Peace,

This is Davon McNeil, checking in for duty. For those of you who truly know me, you know I was on the frontline for many years. For those of you who don't know me, "do the knowledge to my history for yourself. Don't take anything at face value." I didn't just step off the porch and onto the frontline, either. I played my position as a ground soulja for many years and climbed my way up the ranks. What I witnessed out there in the field was pure wickedness, and no young man or woman should ever have to see or experience it. I still get chills at times.

As a direct result of my former way of living. I've spent the past 16 years of my life locked up within a prison house. The life I led prior to entering prison was a life based on ignorance, lies, falsehoods and iniquity. At times, while sitting in this cold and lonely cell, reflecting on my life in the streets, it truly saddens me to realize the savage state-of-mind (mentally) in which I existed. To all of the people who may have been victims of my madness, self-hatred and selfishness, I'm honestly sorry. I did not come out of my mother's womb that way. The lost and destructive individual I became was a manifestation of learned behavior; behavior fed to my pliable young mind at birth and encouraged by my elders and peers.

For me, negative became positive and positive became negative, literally. Prison and attending funerals were normal activities for me while growing up. It was viewed as just a part of the life I was living. Prison and funerals were a part of the culture. There were no positive external forces to compare to my negative way of living... And on September 15, 2003, I was tried and convicted of second degree murder by the courts and my entire life, as I understood it, was about to change. The environment I grew up in (which I was used to) was going to become obsolete.

Over these past 14 years I've come to know, understand, respect and appreciate the law of karma. There is a universal law which governs the entire universe. That law is based on love, peace and happiness. When you observe what takes place within the sky (heavens), you're witnessing all things at peace. Nothing within that celestial realm is out of order. All things up there exist on a harmonious level. It's us earthly beings who exist in a state of constant chaos and confusion. As we strive hard within these dirty streets, going against the natural order and its universal laws, we then begin to cause the law to work against us. The signs are always subtle, at first; maybe a small arrest for trespassing in the hood. But as we continue to travel deeper into debt with the law of nature, the retribution it's going to deliver becomes even greater.

I've come to understand, through experience, that the universe allows no debt to go unpaid. Well, here I sit in prison, paying my debt. I consider myself one of the fortunate ones because many of my peers paid with their lives. I was only able to realize this divine truth by obtaining the knowledge of my true self and who I am as an Original Man (Blackman). As Original people (black) we have a supreme relationship with the universe and everything within it. I will suggest that all who read these pages begin to look within yourselves and seek the greatness which lies within your physical composition. I am speaking of that which I've experienced for myself. There is no mystery to what I'm telling you. You can either accept what I'm giving you or reject it. Just keep in mind: it's your own debt you're building up. No debt goes unpaid! I've spoken on its divine truth. You've been warned...

Positive Education Always Corrects Errors — and that's Peace!

THE STRUGGLE

My dude, ever since that horrible day.. .that day when the white folks put them chrome bracelets (cuffs) on my wrists and read me my rights, it's been nothing but pure hell. That's the only way I can describe it because there is no other definition in the world which can describe the pain I am living. I, literally, live in hell (prison). That shit they talk about, being under the ground, is a mystery to me. I'm speaking about a place of repetitive pain, depression, abandonment, anxiety and some other atrocious shit. My dude, you already know the background story about how my own bloodline (family) declared war against me and put the people (police) on me. Ever since then my life has been reduced to collect calls and the occasional once or twice visit a year from whoever is feeling sorry for me. That's some real sorry shit, my dude.

Muthafuckers visit me out of sympathy, not support. This natural life sentence I'm carrying on my back has caused close friends and females, whom I thought really loved me, to fall by the wayside. This natural life sentence has made me into a fucking circus freak to them. "Step right up and come see little lobster boy" type of shit. People aren't trying to embrace this prison shit. Who am I to blame somebody for not wanting to be a part of this depressing experience? I'm sentenced to natural life in prison; natural fuckin' life. Who wants to get pat- searched and physically violated just to come visit me?

I am the same one who lived my life, while in the free world, running the streets in straight neglect and disregard for all those who truly loved me. Yes, I spent good bread (money) on wifey and the seeds (kids); paid the bills and all that, but what good was all that if I didn't spend quality time with them? The saddest part about the whole thing is that I was hurting my wife and kids. My self-centered ass woke up every single day with one intention: simply doing me, myself, and I. So, to be completely honest with myself, there is no reason I should be expecting support from anyone. I put my street career before my family, simple and plain.

My dude, I'm not even going to get into the details of what my hands have done. I was a fucking savage, my dude. Pure, fucking savage. Check this out...I haven't seen my children in six years. My youngest son does not know who I am. He was born while I was in prison. I failed them, my dude. But I'm going to right my wrongs. My dude, the one person I want to apologize to (and I will never get the chance) is my mom. When I lost her three weeks ago (December 3, 2009), in my panic I inherited all of her pain and stress. I honestly think I had a stroke that day, my dude. The pain in my chest was crazy and my whole right side was pins and needles. The feeling was just crazy, my dude. The worst part about losing my mom is that I don't even know her cause of death. On the line where it says cause of death, it simply says "pending." I don't even know how my mom died, homie.

But on some real shit, homie, I truly believe that my mom died from a broken heart. I put that on everything that I love, my dude. She was only 48 years old, homie. All that shit I put my mom through and this natural life sentence that I got killed my mom, homie. This shit took the only woman who knew me best. She was my everything, my dude. Damn... and these are just my thoughts and feelings for today, December 26, 2009. Only the good Lord knows what tomorrow will bring. I'm going to sign off here but, before I go, let me just say that you've been more than a family to me, my dude. Always keeping it 100% and I love you for that...

Your brother from another,
Shawn G. Jenkins

COME RIDE WITH ME

Okay. Hit the brakes. Now let me put this ink in fifth gear and then allow my thoughts to come to life on this paper for a few seconds. You ready? Listen. Out of the gate, it's death before dishonor. No half-assin' at all. What you see and read from me is what you get. I'm a product of the 80's when it comes to this thing called "the game." At a very young age I inherited some priceless jewels from some real bona fide G's (aka Hood Scholars). I took the bits and pieces, put the puzzle together and was able to see the picture clearly, or so I thought.

See, I learned a whole lot while being trapped within this prison. I learned that all kin ain't kin (family), and all friends ain't friends. When your freedom is snatched away the real loved ones will stay. But after a while even some of them blow away in the wind. Those who said, "I'm here to the end," don't exist anymore. So, for the special few who are still standing tall within your corner, they should be given the utmost respect and honor which they rightfully deserve because we left them to come to prison; they didn't leave us.

Freedom is a special gift which should be cherished to the fullest. Today I awoke with a handful of people still trooping with me and they have been down with me since day one. That was 22 years ago. Check this out. Someone asked me the other day, "Who do you respect more than anything?" I told him, "The game." Listen, the game never lied to me; the game kept it 100% from the start; and the game told me straight up like this: "You can fall in love with me if that's your desire or attempt to get rich off of me, but just remember that I don't give a fuck about you."

The game has no conscience. She has been true to her word and she has never switched up her style on me. From the day I was introduced to her she has remained the same–cold and heartless. Today, I am a father and a husband. My two ladies are the ones who need me the most, so everything that I do is for them. It's bigger than me today. It's a picture which no frame can hold. My ladies know that I love them with all of my heart. But showing and proving it is the real true test. I am blessed in so many ways. Always remember, the game loves no one.

One Luv,
Orange-Man

AGELESS

I used to think that the saying, "Life is what you make it" was a bunch of bullshit. But when I stopped bullshitting the saying came to life. Another saying I could not really understand was, "Misery loves company." I used to think it was my mother's way of keeping me away from the so-called real dudes from my hood. Experience has taught me that through real situations, trials and error, and pain, life is precious, and we only get one shot at it. My mom was dropping some real jewels on me and I refused to admire the beauty within them until now. At times I ask myself why it took an 18-year prison sentence in order for me to realize how great I am. Please understand that this build is not being written to impress you. It's being written to bless you with divine jewels that my teacher has taught me. And in case you're wondering who my teacher is her name is experience.

All of my life I have been told that I'm a product of my environment. I bought into that statement — hook, line and sinker. But today when I hear that statement, it sounds like an excuse for a black man to spew out of his mouth instead of taking responsibility for his actions. The statement gave me a chance to be ignorant, disrespect my community, embarrass my mother, as well as plague my neighborhood with drugs and violence. But today I realize I am not a product of my environment because I need no excuses. Yesterday I was lost. I lacked knowledge of myself and I had no direction. When one lacks knowledge of himself, he doesn't realize he comes from a long line of great kings and queens, and wrapped up within his DNA is that same greatness.

My advice to whoever is reading these words is to slow down and figure out who you truly are. This search for true knowledge may require you to sit in a quiet room or library for an hour each day. But trust me when I tell you, it's a thousand times better than sitting in a cell for 10 to 20 years. If you take my advice, you'll begin to create a path for finding your inner-self and exactly where your life is heading. Always know that you are filled with overflowing potential and you can achieve anything. Over the years while sitting in prison I have witnessed men teach themselves how to draw, speak other languages, cut hair and many other great things. We just need to slow our lives down and tap into that storehouse of divine greatness. Don't wait until you're in prison to slow your life down. Keeping your mind closed will cause you to die. Open it and you have the ability to fly...

Experience...

THE NATURAL ORATOR

The Natural Orator

Dear Reader,

My name is Lincoln Geoffrey Latham, Jr. I am a black man whose soul's power is beginning to manifest and reveal itself daily. And for this awakening I am grateful. I am able to embrace my current situation wholeheartedly. Yet, you ought to know that I find no pleasure being within a physical prison and having such a heavy sentence. But if I can sustain the weight, then is it really heavy? If I can create liberty, am I really confined? The answer is no. What this shows is that through the power of my thoughts, and through the power of my breathing and centralizing my focus on self-development, all situations can be endured if the discipline and strength of the individual in said situation is in full operation.

I have come to know that there is a better side within the black race than what we really show. The better side is the divine ability to activate our supreme will for self-determination through proper health and stability. As original people we literally have the power to birth health and stability from within our physical composition without ingesting our former slave master's diabolical, lab-made poisons. If we would only cultivate the better side within us through analyzing and critiquing our own mind sets, behavior patterns and value systems; study literature that is focused on soul building, knowledge of self and community consciousness; and applying all of the above through honorable and virtuous behavior on a consistent basis. Then that better side will become all that we are, and the worst side will become all that we are not.

Each person must face themselves as they are because the worst prison is the one of internal denial. But on the opposite spectrum, the greatest freedom is receptive awareness because then you can see and receive all things as they are. Once you enter into that supreme state, no rope from any dimension of the world can bind you because you've been awakened to your oneness with the cosmos (the natural arrangement and order of the universe). This divine awakening will allow you to comprehend that the world is your playground and consequently, wherever you exist you're at home. Therefore, structure your home according to your liking.

Build on this and let the building bring out that which is better!

LIFE IS THE REVEALER OF TRUTH

Life is the Revealer of Truth

Nothing reveals the truth like being sentenced to life in prison. You will see the truth about your friendships, who is real, who is fake, and who had an abundance of love, or endless hate, for you in secret. You will see if the love which significant others had for you was the type of love that was real; the type that could stand up under extreme duress and extreme stress.

Could it stand the test of time, or was the term "I love you" merely words with no feelings behind them? You'll get to check the truth regarding family. They are the people you once felt you would give your life for: mom, dad, brothers, sisters, aunts, uncles, cousin, grandma and grandpa. You would have given your life for them at one time and here you are, not dead at all, and you can't get a visit, card, letter, money order...nothing! As it turns out, some family members were no better than the fake friends.

You'll see the truth about your prison environment, the CO's, the administration, the convicts, the inmates, the volunteers and the staff. You'll see those who do their time and those who allow time to do them. You'll see men with strong minds who learn and master complex things of life as if these things are mere toys. You'll also witness men with weak minds who chase young boys and wear lipstick. You will see men who will not sacrifice their dignity or character in the imaginary sand they drew with their lives. You'll see men who entered prison as 17-year old boys and are now in their 50's, 60's and 70's with full heads of grey hair or no hair at all. You'll see men whose minds have cracked and now they run full speed to the medication line.

But most important of all, if you take the proper time, you'll find out about yourself. You will also find out that you've been wearing many masks which do not belong to you. You'll reflect on all the mistakes you've made based on immaturity, ego and pride. You'll hear every single warning that anyone has ever uttered to you and replay them within your mind as you close your eyes and meditate on your life's journey. I'm 14 years into a 15 to life sentence and so far my truth is this: I have learned more about myself and life in these 14 years I have been in prison than I ever could in the 26 years I spent in the streets chasing a dream. My motto is, "God gave me two ears and one mouth for a reason." You'll never hear lifesaving jewels if you're always running your mouth, talking about foolishness.

We all have strengths and we all have weaknesses. Strive hard to activate off of your strengths. It makes life a lot easier. When someone shows you the truth about themselves, accept it. Then take your time to decide if you want their truth in your life because the truth is the truth. It never changes regardless of whom or what. If you embrace it, you can deal with it. Whatever the truth may be...

Always one vision.
Charles F. Bogues

YOU'LL NEVER KNOW UNTIL YOU'VE BEEN THERE

You will never know what prison is like until you have been here fighting this war. We are on the frontline every single day with these devils. We fight for freedom every day. We fight for better food, lower security, parole and we fight for our sanity. The war never stops. Prison is a living hell. You're alive but being tortured within a modern-day slave plantation.

The ones who care are the same ones who would care about you if you were dead and gone (family).

Do not be fooled by your captors. Their sole purpose is to utilize you as a tool and as a slave. You are an animal in their eyes. Check your history. Once upon a time they considered us three-fifths of a human being. And there is no rehabilitation going on in prison unless you are rehabilitating yourself. Where is the rehabilitation for my comrades who are doing natural life and 15 years to life sentences? I've got comrades in prison who were sentenced to 15 years to life bids and have been in prison for 35 years.

We are being warehoused within these hellholes for the government's maximum profit. Wake up and realize you can't win within that negative lifestyle called "the game." No justice! No peace!

One love,
Mizz

LIFE OF A LIFER

Prison is a lot of things to a lot of people. But in all prisons, none is without love for something or someone. We adapt, fight, suffer, struggle and hope upon the continued existence of those bonds of love which provide us strength and give our lives some meaning or purpose of his continued existence. Is life truly greater than death, just for the mere existence of being alive? Or is the meaning of life, a life you are alive in its living existence? Know thy life. Then to that life, be true.

Mourn me not when I am gone.

One day of this life was one too long.

I gave the best I had to give.

To just exist is a life I will not live.

From the soul of Brother Smitty,

Hubert Smith

1978 until my last stand...

FAMOUS QUOTES

1. For every moment of one's existence, one is growing into more or retreating into less.

2. The primary and most beautiful of nature's qualities is motion.

3. Be a lamp or a lifeboat or a ladder. Help someone's soul heal. Walk out of your house like a shepherd.

4. It's not for the moment you are stuck that you need courage, but for the long uphill climb back to sanity and faith and security.

5. Just throw away all thoughts of imaginary things and stand firm in that which you are.

6. Suppose you scrub your ethical skin until it shines, but inside there is no music. Then what?

7. Most of us are about as eager to be changed as we were to be born and go through our changes in a similar state of shock.

8. Surviving meant being born over and over.

9. Be strong then and enter into your own body. There you have a solid place for your feet.

10. If you want the truth, I'll tell you the truth: listen to the secret sound, the real sound which is inside of you.

11. The meeting of two personalities is like the contact of two chemical substances. If there are any reactions both are transformed.

12. The changes in your life must come from the impossibility to live otherwise than according to the demands of our conscience.

13. We can never go back again; that much is certain.

14. One is happy as a result of one's own efforts. Once one knows the necessary ingredients of happiness, simple tastes, a certain degree of courage, self-denial to a point, love of work, and above all, a clear conscience.

15. You must do the thing you think you cannot do.

16. It is good to have an end to journey towards, but it is the journey which matters in the end.

17. What most of us want is to be heard; to communicate.

18. You need only claim the events of your life to make yourself yours.

19. We are shaped and fashioned by what we love.

20. Keep growing quietly and seriously throughout your whole development.

I was told years ago by one of my aunts, "Always seek the dead trees that feed the mind." What she meant was, always read books to educate your mind because knowledge will free you.

Famous Quotes M.T.

REAL WISDOM FOR THE STREETS

Yo "Vee," true story right here. You know me, so you know I'm keeping it 100% when I say that I know mad heads; some older, some my age and some even younger than myself. I know cats that eat well off of slinging "D" (dope and every other kind of drug). I know cats that drop stacks on whips (cars), on freezing chains and some more shit. I also know mad hungry cats stalking them muthafuckers I named above, that don't have any problem warming up that steel when they catch 'em sleeping. I also know plenty of dudes that posted crazy bails and they're considered hood stars in the minds of youngins. Now, I have fallen into one of those categories at times in my life and I must admit that while playing in the streets I failed to see the pain that I was causing my loved ones.

I got in the game late and I've been losing ever since. If I was winning, or had won, I wouldn't be writing in this book. I've been in prison for 15 years now and during that time I've lost my mother, failed to be there for my kids, and I have grandkids who only know me from behind these prison walls. That's crazy! But today I'm older, wiser and more mature. I have applied the math to a lot of things while in prison. I've asked myself on many occasions, "Damn, have I wasted my entire life?" The answer is "no." My life is what it is and can only get better. I have a lot to be grateful for. There are things I wouldn't change for nothing in this world, family being number one. But there are many things I'm sorry for. For starters, forcing my mom to hold me down in courtrooms and hospitals; sorry for all the times she worried about me when I stayed out late or all night; and sorry for all the times she found drugs, guns and shells which I stashed in her house. But I am most sorry for not being by her side during her last days on this earth. I'm also sorry that my son and daughter have to come visit their father in this hellhole (prison). And I'm sorry that I was not in the crowd at their graduations. Damn Vee, it hurts writing this. Homie, that street life, thug life cost me my whole life and all I can say is "damn." But I gotta stay focused. No time to stress about my sorry ass. What's done is done. I gotta make sure my son doesn't follow my footsteps and start selling drugs, carrying guns or kill a muthafucker and end up in a cell next door to mine. Vee, you know we see that shit every day; father and son in prison. Vee, I worry about that shit all the fucking time, real talk. That would cause my heart to bleed. I heard stories about you and your pop being in the same prison a few times. Is that real talk, Vee? We'll build on that later.

I wonder if someone would have told me about the things, I would go through by living the fast life in the streets, would my life have turned out differently? Well, we will never know the answer to that question with this natural life sentence on my back. But I will spend my last days telling the youth the truth. Vee, we gotta holla at them early. This prison shit is honestly for the birds and my wings have been clipped. Oh, it's a true story! Vee stay a good brother. Stay on point, comrade.

Stay trying to make the youth understand. God bless you, Vee.

Big Brother Sunshine, 100

NO EXPLANATION

I don't need to tell you what I've done. I'm not proud of it. I try to forget about it as much as possible, even if it seems as though I never can. As I write these words please bear with me because my mind travels. I don't like when someone says to me, "I love you." Those words seem to roll out of people's mouths too easily. It's a cliché. Everyone says it to everyone these days. It has lost its spark. Now, if you say, "I need you," that's something special. To need is powerful. It says I cannot live without you.

At times, while shaving, I think how easy it would be to just make a quick slice, hit the vein and slowly feel life escape from me. All of my pain, heartache, sadness and remorse would simply fade into black. Then I would know the secrets of the afterlife. Maybe a great adventure awaits me there and I could take that journey with just a quick flick of the wrist. I could travel to another reality where I'm not considered one of the worst human beings on the planet — a "murderer." But that would be quitting; giving up. And one rule which I live by is to never quit under any circumstances. I will not be defined by the worst moment of my life. I refuse to become what others label me. So, I keep shaving and the moment passes.

Honestly, what is true reality? The weight of a life bid makes you question your own sanity. When you read about yourself in the newspaper and how people describe one moment in time, a moment filled with so much pain and suffering that it feels as if there is too much to go around. It's like a river flooding and taking everything with it. How many lives have been ruined by that one act of stupidity and violence? Is someone who is capable of such stupidity and violence redeemable? You have to believe in miracles. Those of us who have been sentenced to natural life in prison are miracles. Those of us who bear fruit are divine; apple trees growing in the desert; something that is not supposed to happen in a hostile environment — such as prison.

Peace,

Mende Semedo

TO THE YOUNG QUEEN

May your life be filled with health and may your days be filled with accomplished dreams. My life has been filled with trials and tribulations. Some deserved, some unfair but nonetheless, they're mine to bear. I extend to you the only thing that I feel is worthy. It is not advice or rules. It's love. Little lady, love yourself long before you love another. Love your future because it's tomorrow. Love your parents and all your family because they are all that you have, and they are your roots. Love your community because they are your world. Love God because He is everything and created everything.

I extend to you the gift of time. Time is all yours. It can be a blessing or a curse. Use it wisely and cherish every waking moment. Young queen, this is your life; your lot within this universe. Fulfill your dreams and destiny and manifest your greatness within the world. Everything else will follow. Don't live for tomorrow, cherish today. Enjoy being you. Enjoy your youth. Not with a crazy sense of excitement, but with a thoughtful use of your abilities, your potential and your great mind.

With these words of wisdom, I bid you farewell. Peace and blessings. Young queen, seeing your bright smile out in the visiting room with your father allows me to know that the outside world is blessed to have you within its realm. God bless you, young lady.

Live life to the fullest,

Herby C.

LIVE FROM THE AVE

I want to touch on our choices and the fact that after we make them, they make us. On December 6, 2002, my life as a free man in the free world came to an end. However, adversity breeds true character, so I found true freedom within this adversity. I was into everything except a casket, good brother. The drug game had me in the free world speeding. I neglected so much and too many to reveal in one lifetime. I can never replace all the time I've lost. Therefore, I've got to cherish the time that I've got left because there's one thing prison has taught me: you can lose your life at any moment.

I truly cherish meeting you (my very first cellmate upstate). I found freedom within you, your struggle and all the wise words you've blessed me with. You are beyond your years, brother. I believe in your new mental state and I know you will change many lives for the better. We've all committed some wrongs. But what separates us is our next choice. Our next choice will reveal the true meaning of a man. One might ask the question, "What makes a man, a man?" I would have to honestly say, "His actions." Peace brother Vee. The love and respect I have for you is through the sky. I wish you and your family the best of wishes. Teach them youth, brother.

One love,

L.O.

THE LIE

I was told that I could get money in the game. I was told that the game would be good to me as long as I kept it real and played by the rules. I was told that (the game) was a fast way out of the hood. I was told that all I had to do was be loyal to the game. I was told that I would be able to make shit happen. I was told that it was a way of life for us. I was taught how to cook, chop and bag up crack at an early age. I was told that money was king. I was told about all of the wonderful things money would bring. I was told all of the above by family and so-called friends.

Today I sit in prison with a life sentence. I realize that I was led astray and lied to. I fell for the trick that so many of my peers fell for, and it seems we're all either in prison or dead. I honestly can't blame those who told and taught this bullshit because I now realize they were told and taught the same lies. Many people told me I was a king, full of greatness and intelligence. They saw in me what I did not see in myself. And before I end this message, I would like to share with you a quote from Nelson Mandela which states, "Our deepest fear is not that we are inadequate. Our deepest fear is that we are powerful beyond measure."

Peace,
"C"

SELF

I believe that one's life is dictated by one's own philosophy about what he believes his own life is, or what he believes it should be. There's life, and then there's life; one you live and one you do. The choice is all yours. Just remember, nothing comes to a sleeper but a dream and after you awake, even that is gone.

E. G. Wright

FATHERLESS SON'S

Peace to the reader who has taken the time to read my thoughts which I've turned into matter. I was raised by true lies. What I have come to understand about that statement (raised by true lies) is that the people who raised me thought that what they were teaching me was the truth. Therefore, I can't be mad at my elders (mentors) because they were lied to, also. Thus, the cycle continued. Prison is a part of the streets and we all called her "wifey." Damn, I raised my first son to be just like me. He was a legend in his stroller at eight months old: rocking Guess™ and Nike™. I can use this time to write about how my "wifey" left me for dead, but it's deeper than her right now. I wish her the best.

This is about my sons; my flesh and blood; my young kings. Listen my young kings, if you ever get a chance to read these words, I am sorry for being absent in your lives. I saw you (oldest son) enter into this world on that cold December night. Wow, I made life. You were so pure and innocent as I once was. So, son, please don't be like me. I beg you to be better than me. Those streets got me sentenced to 18 years in prison; 18 years I'm going to lose out of your life.

I used to always tell people, "I don't give a fuck if I die because my son is alive." Now, I realize how ignorant I was because I've always cared about living. I was just mentally lost from my true self.

But son, I've been fed the right foods (knowledge of self) to pass on to you and your brothers and sisters. I want to see you all live your lives. We will break the curse so that none of you fall victim to the false lies that I thought were the truth. I learned the hard way. So please learn from my mistakes. A smart man makes them (mistakes) and a wise man learns from them. A wise man taught me to never take anything at face value. He taught me that it's knowledge before wisdom and that understanding is the best part (you, my son). He said, "I had to get right with myself in order to be right with you." Son, this wise man put a book in my hand; no money, no drugs and no guns. It was a book, my son, which is food for thought. So, if this same book ever reaches your hands, I pray that you're within a college dorm room reading its pages.

To everyone who took the time to break food in this book remember this, they trap our bodies, but they can never trap our minds. We're forever free. We just adapt to time...

Peace God, you helped the blind (me) see/cee. Thank you, Vee

P.S. I still remember the math on how many inches there is on our planet: 12 trillion, 478 billion, 118 million, 400 thousand inches...Wow!

Chunky Boy (aka) Troy Clemons

CELL TIME

Prefer - to choose; more desirable. I preferred the fast life even though I was conditioned to believe that life was the right path. I knew the debt I would have to someday pay. Do I regret it? No. Everyone's story is different. Pain to me is defined in this meaning: when you see that loved one's face, "my mom" with tears running down it; blood shot eyes; and bags underneath her eyes so black even a plastic surgeon can't remove them. It's pain to see my mom on her knees, praying to a mystery God who only listens.

Chose - (verb) to decide on; to pick out and select. I chose to play the game and lost my freedom, my girl, my so-called friends and even some of my family. I guess the pain I delivered was too much for the so-called thugs to bear. I chose for them to take the witness stand against me which in turn got me this 15-to-life prison sentence. If you love someone or something, don't make them choose. My ways and actions made people have to choose. Whether it was good or bad I was the cause of it all. One of the best quotes I ever heard states, "Laugh now, cry later." I hope that anyone reading this will never have to experience the full meaning of that quote.

Blessed be the Journey,

The President!!!

SOLO IS MY MOVEMENT

Peace,

I promise to remember what feeds my soul and will bring more of it into my life. I've been doing this sentence since the age of 14. I'm 28 years old today. I was told by the OG's that, "If you allow it, prison can kill your soul, take away your self-worth and your self-respect." For the first eight years that wisdom from the OG's was my reality. Within the first eight years I lost family, friends and so-called girlfriends. One day I woke up in this hell (prison) and had no one. I was all by myself. The pain of not having people you love in your life runs deep. But I knew I had to create my own path and become a better man and the only person who was responsible for making that happen was me.

While on this mission to find myself, I met some of the strongest and smartest men doing the exact same thing. It's sad but some of those men are also writing their stories for this book. We're all searching for our true selves. Some of these men I consider my family. Why?

Because these men helped me understand my greatness at a time in my life when I thought I was worthless. Today, I fully understand that the people who truly love you are the ones who want to see you grow into a productive member of society. Yes,

I was sentenced to 15 to life, but I refuse to let this sentence kill my soul or my mind. The prison has my physical body but my mind belongs to me. Vee, I want to thank you for allowing me to share my story within your book. I see your vision. Keep up the good work. Our youths need to hear our truths.

"If I am not for myself, then who will be?

If not now, then when?

I strive to be the man I want to be, free"

-" E Cabesa"

CHECKMATE, YOUR MOVE

Peace Divine Mind,

Some say life is a game of chess. I beg to differ and say life is no game at all. However, in the event that I'm wrong, and it is a game, you've got to have knowledge of the cipher before you play the game. Let me do the knowledge so that you can wisdom. Chess is a game invented in Russia (some say Prussia) possibly as early as the 11th or 12th century. The name of the game was pronounced "Shekmatta" which is where we get the word, checkmate. The reason the king can move only one square at a time is because when the kings went to war in those days, they had to take their entire treasure chest with them—since it consisted of precious stones—because banks did not exist. The game was patterned on world domination. When the king was gone the queen was free to do as she wished and roam the kingdom. This is why she moves in any direction and is the most powerful piece on the board. The bishop was originally a sail-ship.

The reason the piece is only moved at an angle is because it's symbolic of a sail catching the crosswinds in order to travel. However, the Catholic Church was appalled that a game based on world domination did not include them. Thus, the sail-ship is known as the bishop.

Now, in the real cipher, the king is the original man (Black Man). The original man today is burdened with the ills of society and the stigma placed upon him by the devil. Hence, he can hardly move and when he does, he hardly comes up. He hustles in a drug game designed by the devil. He works in a tax-infested, minimum wage game designed by the devil. He studies in a school game designed by the devil. Yet, he's god! Meanwhile, the queen is out in the cipher trying to fend for herself. She's roaming in the wilderness because her man/god is either locked up or hasn't mastered one of the devil's many designed games which were created to keep the original man down.

She, in turn, reaches out for one of the government assistance handouts which, coincidently, provide her with more than her man/god can. But that's because the devil knows she's "the most important factor for good economics." The devil knows that if he doesn't provide for her he'll spoil good economics because she can't provide him with new baby boys/gods for him to subject to his many designed evils.

This is why the Catholic Church strategically placed themselves directly beside the king and queen as bishop in place of the sail-ship. White pieces vs. black pieces and the white pieces always move first. There are 64 squares on a chess board. 6+4 borns = 10. Like I said, you've got to have knowledge of the cipher to play the game.

My name is W.F. Muhammad!

>Decipher Self First
>"I Prime Absolute"

*In self lies all mathematics...

AS SALAM WALAIKUM

As I look around, I see young, old, black, white, tall, short, fat, thin, son, father, grandfathers, juniors, seniors, etc. What do we all have in common? We have all been taken from our loved ones, family and friends. We're all doing time. Some of us will never see our loved ones as "free men" ever again; and some of us will. I never took the time out to think about that side of this thing we call "The Game." It's really not a game at all. But now that I'm in prison, and forced to see reality, all I see is pain and empty eyes.

Now, all I have is time to "think." I also have a lot of time to do. So, before you become me, take time out to clearly think about what you're about to do with your next step because it may be your next step into prison. And prison is where the walking dead dwells. Real talk! Think, think, think... Only you know what to do for you. All I'm saying is — think about your life first. Your next move could cost you everything, including your life...or someone else's.

Mr. Ingram aka "Philly"

LIVE

Life. What does it mean when the State hands it to you? Well, it means a complete renovation of your heart, mind and soul; a complete transformation process which takes years to begin. It's almost like a transparent awakening which lifts your unconsciousness up slowly to your consciousness, allowing a meeting for the very first and last time. This is a battle for life…

In prison you become one of two things: 1) you either begin to discover that you are a great man with many hidden talents and you happened to wander the darkest path without so much as a shred of light or guidance, or 2) you opt to go hard in war for the hell of it because within your mind you have nothing to lose. Well, allow me to enlighten you from the perspective of doing a natural life sentence. I wouldn't suggest the second choice because that's the path which leads to death and destruction. You'll end up in DDU—which is a prison within prison—or you'll get shipped out of state. Like I said, you'll end up dead.

I owe a lot of gratitude to every veteran convict who helped me make some very wise choices by sharing, not just their love and respect, but also their knowledge, wisdom and understanding with me when I was lost. Without these men I wouldn't have focused on this fight for my life. I am fighting for my life, literally! Without these wise men I would be focused on destroying. So, in essence, my life wasn't taken. It was given…thank you!

Carlos Gomes
aka
The Big Boss

Vee, thank you for allowing me the opportunity to express myself within the pages of your book. Keep striving, Comrade.

AUR-NUR: THE LIGHT

In the name of God, the beneficent, the merciful...

On March 27th of this year (2010), I was asked a question. The question was, "What is it like being in prison?" My response was perceived as me being impersonal by the author of said question. So this time I will try to respond in a more personal manner. But, in order to understand what prison is like for me, you must close your eyes and strive to detect my mental frequency because prison is a different place for each individual trapped within its walls. No two prisoners view their prison experience the same way. There is an old song which I hold dear to my heart which says, "Nobody knows the trouble I've seen; nobody knows my sorrows." That's my prison. No matter how much you listen there's always a new story to tell. So how can you truly understand unless you've experienced it for yourself?

My prison is filled with thoughts of the past and what I could've done with my life. As far back as I can remember my life's dream was to become a big rap star. I've shared my songs and poetry with thousands of people over the years and they're always amazed at my abilities. I often look in the mirror and ask myself, "Is it too late? Is my dream just a dream because of my incarceration, or will my story be more entertaining because of this experience? I've often heard that the more pain that you experience the better you are at writing. I'll have to admit it's the truth. But that is just my opinion. Fortunate is the writer in my position, huh?

I wrote a song called "Nobody Knows" because when speaking on the subject of prison there's no other fitting statement. If you have not experienced prison, you'll never know. Every man sitting behind these walls have their own problems and things they're stressing over. I've met guys who have lost their mothers while in prison and you'd never know unless they revealed it to you. And on the flip side I know guys whose wives have left them, and these men have lost their sanity. Plus, society has taught us that men don't stress and damn sure don't cry. Men have become masters at hiding their true feelings. Do you know what it's like to sleep, cook, eat, wash up, piss, shit, pray, wash dishes and write letters in an 8x10 cell occupied by you and another man? Can you relate? I shit and piss four feet from where I lay my head.

My prison is where you go to sleep before you're tired; where you pull your blanket over your head even when you're not cold. My prison is a place where I try to obtain food for thought even though I've witnessed some men bite off too much and choke...never to take a bite again. I've learned to take very small bites and chew slowly. I eat just enough to sustain me for nourishment so that I can grow to a healthy level. My prison is where I've come to fully understand the saying, "Ignorance is bliss." My prison is a place where your demons are as real as your flesh. They're there whether your eyes are opened or closed. My prison is real. What lies behind us and what lies before us are tiny matters. It's what lies within us that matters. Stay free.

Nuri Muhammad aka

Born Lyte-Al Nur

QUIET STORM

Years ago, I heard that the only things in prison are corpses which refuse to lie down. At times, during my 20 years in prison. I've seen exactly how that statement is relevant. I've also seen prison as a game yard for the living, including me. There have been times when I've seen prison as a maternity ward where in the midst of hopelessness, fear and pain a spark has been given hope, love and purpose. I've seen men manifest pure greatness within an environment which breeds constant hate. I've witnessed men who were complete savages create new realities for themselves and operate in a righteous manner on a daily basis.

Men who were sentenced to life were no longer doing life but living their lives. These men were sharing their wisdom with each other and finding ways to teach each other how to survive in prison. They were striving to elevate each other within the confines of their existence. It has been through observing and listening to these men which has helped me to become focused on living life as opposed to serving this life sentence handed down to me by the courts. I can honestly say I've been reborn. It's a strange sight to see corpses walking and talking amongst the living (smile). I pray that if you ever see me walking dead again, you'll breathe life into me.

Vee, this book may be a spark for the mentally dead.

Brother J.P.

James H. Pearson, III

CARRY YOUR CROSS

P.E.A.C.E.

Jesus wept. I laughed. People pray. These are some of the responses when faced with pressure. I feel as though Jesus wept because He didn't trust in His ability as God to save His people. So He said, "I'll be back," like the Terminator. People pray because they have been conditioned to rely on everyone but themselves. I laugh because I not only declare to be God, I realize this divine reality. I loved my hell and came out right. I cannot give this realization through words from my mouth. We all have to love our own hell; love being the highest elevation of understanding. What I can tell you is this — learn all the science of everything and know that everything has a name (vibration) and as matter it will answer to.

Although I've been sentenced to life without the possibility of parole, as God, I will not spend more than five years in this situation. For I say, "be," and it is. Also, acknowledging the fact that I write my own history in advance, I realize that I am here for a reason. Writing this jewel is part of that cause. The effect is the evolution of people. So, in closing, learn and study about yourself for I am; so you'll be...

Peace, Ptah Amen Hetop, Freedom Love

Allah, Isreal Zodok El Eloh,

Lord of Death, Leonard J. Jackson

TRIALS AND TRIBULATIONS

Listen, this is what I'm writing to show and prove that I am the truth. I came into this world about 50 years ago and I never really made my mark in the world because I was too busy running wild in the streets. Today I feel it's my time to truly shine and the good which I will do will reach all those who are spiritually and mentally blind, like I was. The knowledge which I am responsible for sharing is not only for the head, but also for the heart. So, for me, life is just about to start. I am no leader. I'm here to respond to individuals' needs rather than their faults.

I am not afraid to admit I need to listen more and get a better understanding of myself and life. I evaluate what my life has become because of my ignorance. I'm constantly seeking higher ground to walk on after existing so low. But I still need to do some mental work on myself. I have learned that if the clouds are full of rain, they empty themselves onto the earth. Also, if a tree falls to the north or the south, the tree shall lie in the place where it fell until a greater force comes along to utilize it for a better purpose.

Some people tell me I have more stored within me than I give myself credit for. But I've learned that the humble man will always catch the eyes of many. As for violence, I use to carry it in my left pocket. But today I have reduced my behavior by taking the plug out of the socket. I'm more focused today than I have ever been in my life. I have allowed myself to grow by releasing myself from inner demons which were holding me captive within my own fear of success. In my past life there was always someone in the way — me.

I would also like to use my time in this book to admit I've allowed "heroin" to mentally and physically abuse me in the past, but each passing day I strive to conquer the beast. Changes are being made and progress is showing. My wife and I have become as one and she's my biggest advocate for change. I feel really good within my heart and mind. I only ask that all who read my words to become wise and know you're blessed by the best: God. Constantly feed your mind the proper mental sustenance and it will grow strong.

Vee keep doing your good work for the youth.

One Love,
Boyd Price
aka Big Lou

I'M SORRY LITTLE LADY

Little lady, I'm sorry; I left you unprotected in that evil, cold world;

At your birth I promised never to leave daddy's little girl (damn).

I watched quietly as your mother nourished you from her breast;

I still cherish memories of wiping your throw-up off of my bare chest (smile).

I'm sorry, Little Lady; your first night home from the hospital I wouldn't let you out of my sight; Your mother kept telling me to relax, that you were going to be alright.

Baby, you wouldn't remember this, but I surely do;

I bought you your first pair of sneakers — they were Nikes: white, pink and blue (smile).

I'm sorry, Little Lady; I remember at one of your doctor's appointments you cried so hard and loud because the doctor gave you a shot in your chubby little leg;

Baby girl, I swear, seeing you in tears gave me visions of knocking that doctor upside his head.

I'm sorry, Little Lady; you grew up so fast and I've

missed so much. And as your father it was my duty to be there to clean that first scrape on your knee and to kiss it all better;

But no, I chose them streets; it got me sending my love through prison letters (damn).

I'm sorry, Little Lady; for the past 12 1/2 years I've watched you grow up through pictures;

I missed your first birthday; I missed your very first steps and I never heard you say "Dada" (damn).

I'm sorry, Little Lady; Juel, please forgive me for leaving you in the world all alone;

I was lost from my true self. I was so far from home.

I remember the very first time you asked me, "Daddy, when are you coming home?"

My heart broke, and I cried while holding that prison phone.

Today you're a lot older and the world has gotten much colder;

We don't speak as much as we did in the past and I haven't seen your beautiful face in almost a year.

I'm sorry, Little Lady; it's my own fault I'm here in prison;

I love you. I love you. I love you. Baby girl,

I left you unprotected in that evil and cold world;

At your birth I promised to never leave daddy's little girl. I'm sorry Little Lady...

I love you, Juel!!! Daddy

DAMN YOU PRISON

Truly, prison is proof that slavery never ended. It has just adjusted to the times; evolving in such a way that it now appears to be appealing to those held captive mentally, and those dumb enough to glorify its wicked existence. There is a war going on and war is never designed to be fun, especially when it's a war against you. Blood stains on the concrete and corpses by the wayside mixed with dirty syringes. Doors kicked off the hinges by the police and the rest of the slave masters are avengers. This is a whole lot of crime and destruction that our kids have to witness and walk by on a daily basis. By the time they reach school in the mornings you can only imagine what's going on in their young minds.

It's twisted! It's chaotic! Just take a look within your own mind. Our minds have been tampered with by wickedly wise scientists who taught us how to eat the wrong foods mentally and physically when we were babies. As a young child I was force-fed lie after lie by my elders who were also tricked and deceived by the wickedly wise. If I knew then what I know now the cycle would not have been able to continue to slowly etch its poison into the very fabric of my being only to be perpetuated by my actions, casting a stigma on myself and my people, thus placing a huge burden on the generation following me. These youths came to me for answers and guidance and all that I could give them was what was given to me. I gave a bunch of lost and misguided youths the same code of ethics passed down to me. At one time these ethics were something to live by. To die by. Just like I did. No questions asked. You simply ride for the cause.

How tragic and reckless was that? All I did was create more mental slaves. I did Jim Crow's dirty work. We keep the dirty work alive by killing off each other and keeping our communities in constant fear. They no longer need to hang us because we're hell-bent on killing each other and ourselves for sport. Even when a wise brother or sister from our struggle strives to educate and teach us something, we call them a sell-out. We question who they're trying to imitate when they speak articulately. We tell them speaking that way is for white people.

Really, how ignorant can we be? Today, we're willing to take penitentiary chances by believing what the rapper, Nas, said: "Real Niggaz bust in broad daylight." Don't we see what is being done to us? We're being led astray by rappers who are being paid millions of dollars to perpetuate a plan designed by the wickedly wise to destroy us. Do you think Nas would tell his son to bust his gun in broad daylight? Hell no!

None of this happened overnight. This was (and is) a slow, thought out, methodical and wicked plan put into existence by the same ones responsible for bringing our ancestors across the Atlantic Ocean to be held captives as slaves over 450 years ago. Gradual dissemination has brought you, me and many others to the brink of self-destruction with a deep resentment for our black brothers, mothers, fathers and even our children. We're doing everything we possibly can to project the hate we have for our own black skin onto those who look just like us. Now is our time to begin a new process of mental revolution from the lower realms of hell (the streets) into a higher state of existence. It is our duty to lead our people back to whence we came. Remind our people that at one time we were kings and queens. We're still kings and queens. We just have to give the slave master back his state of mind which is keeping us trapped within these modern- day slave plantations (prison).

Many of us have already taken that journey back to the land of our divine selves and are helping many others see the light (truth) about themselves. We will once again stand tall on the mountaintop. As it states within the good book (Bible), "The last shall be first, and the first shall be last." My people, we will be victorious! Vee, you're one of those brothers who I respect because you see the challenges which lie ahead. Yet you choose to take them head-on without shying away from your responsibility; your responsibility to our black people who are lost mentally in the wilderness of North America. You recognize the order we must follow in leading our people out of the darkness...

Stay strong, Comrade. We owe this fight to our sons and daughters so soulja on, Vee!

Peace,
-Jason Robinson
aka TY

LOST AND NOW FOUND

Listen, from birth I was fed the wrong foods mentally as well as physically, damn, look at what these dirty streets have done to me.

I never told this to anyone, so please don't laugh,

me and my little brothers had to heat up water in order to take a bath.

At night I would roam them streets to drag home a piece of meat,

just so my mother's three young cubs would have something decent to eat.

My nights were oh-so-cold!

Have you ever had to sleep by the stove? I did.

They ask me why I sold drugs and clutched that Glock.

I looked them in their eyes and asked, "Where was your Pops?"

My dad was where I stand before you today, and if I'm not mistaken it was 15 years and a day.

Who could I talk to? There was nobody home.

My mother was at the clinic getting her daily dose of methadone.

Being the oldest of three boys my little brothers would never understand, what it felt like being 13 years old, taking on the duties of a grown man.

Stop! Now bear witness to me in the penitentiary:

The first seven years spent searching for what a wise man told me was buried within me. The eighth year I found the truth. Everything became clear to me.

I understood why I was created and what I had to do.

Enlighten my people; tell the truth to the youths.

It all made sense now, why I went through trials and tribulations.

So, I would learn to appreciate self-education.

Now, listen to me intently because this is a jewel:

You must learn to love the hell you go through in order to come out of it right.

Believe me my people it's going to be a struggle and fight.

You may ask, "Who is the struggle and fight going to be with?" Look in the mirror and meet your opponent!!

Peace is the way of the righteous,
Honorable: Davon McNeil

Righteous: Divine Victory Allah

YOUNG QUEEN, YOU'RE DIVINELY BLESSED

Peace Queen,

I acknowledged you since you were a young seed and it's an honor and a privilege to add on. The dart I have for you is that the true master is consciousness. I mean true consciousness, not simply being awake. I'm talking about the consciousness which never sleeps. The part of you which is aware of your consciousness. There's a part of you that's always there; always consistent. That part represents your true self. It's the part which connects you to God! That's who you got to get in touch with...

Your brother and servant.
Justice A - Z Muhammad

FRONTLINE SOULJA

Peace,

I have had many experiences during the course of my existence. Having grown up in Baltimore during the Civil Rights Movement and witnessed as well as having been involved in the riots, protests, etc., I learned that only through hard work, education and strong commitments can we as a people achieve respect and equal (just) rights. I also fought in Vietnam where I had first-hand knowledge of the extent to which the U.S. Government will go for political and economic gain. Innocent men, women and children were killed to prove a point; that this U.S. Government would sacrifice men's lives at any cost even though they knew they were fighting a lost cause. It was at that juncture in my life that I took an oath to fight for me, my family and my people, using whatever means necessary. I have studied the teachings of Garvey, Lumumba, Nkumba, Malcolm, Elijah Muhammad, Mao, Che, Stokely, H. Rap Brown and Gandhi. I've read the Qur'an, Bible, Metu Neter and other material and spiritual literature to make a connection between myself and God.

Throughout my 37 years of false (unjust) incarceration I've been on the frontline of our struggle. I've been housed in some of the most secure prisons in the U.S., both State and Federal.

Prison has taught me how to use time to serve me and my cause. In order to properly help my family and others, I must prepare myself to be able to deal with any given situation throughout my journey through life. We as men control our own destiny. I have used the traditional education system to serve me and my interest. Man can accomplish whatever he/she desires. Nothing worth having comes without working hard to get it. We must be willing to make sacrifices and be able to stand on our demonstrations. Always look within self for the

answers to solving your problems. No one knows you better than you know yourself. The Kingdom of Heaven lies within you. Free your mind. Fear no man!

Peace,
Dini Zulu Kamau
aka Efrid Brown, Jr

R.I.P. 1950-2016

ECONOMICS

Peace Brother Vee,

For as long as I can remember I was always in a position where I had to provide for myself and family. Like most of us I took the sucker's bet and gambled with my life by taking the street route. Selling drugs and violence seemed like a sure bet until I crapped out. I woke up and found myself in prison with a life sentence. So, I sucked up this prison reality and turned this place into a college for higher learning. I learned Islam, patience, love and respect. I also learned responsibility which led me to learn and master business (economics). Through the study of economics, I learned how to hustle legally and still make drug-dealing profits. It all depends on how much you start with. Don't worry if you only start with a little. Patiently give yourself five years and by then you should have made enough to make you them big returns.

I flip stacks, fuck CDs, money market accounting, mutual funds and bonds. At least in the beginning stages your returns will be there, but they'll be extremely low. Learn the market for yourself so that you don't have to depend on someone else controlling your money. Those big named companies like to say all kinds of fancy words in order to get you to allow them control of your paper (money) as if though you're not smart enough; or even smarter when it comes to management of your money and affairs. Many of us fall for their tricks and get less return on our money. Understanding money allows you to make it no matter what circumstances arise. In some situations, those other outlets regarding money can be utilized. Why I chose to speak on economics? Well, it's money that we as people don't have enough of and we make deadly decisions striving to get it. Therefore, I figured I would tell the world about it so that anyone who wants to can learn as I did.

The root of our problem no longer exists. The problem which comes from this is that we do so much to leave behind a money-cushion for our children so that they can be stress-free. But it cost us, and them, dearly because they no longer have the desire to fend for themselves.

Passing wealth onto people or children with no understanding of money is a very foolish idea. It leads to a path we worked so hard to get away from — poverty. We must push our family to learn the game of economics and money management. They must be able to build off the foundation you leave behind and expand it for the next generation following behind them.

Listen to this business parable: A man has land with a house he owns with a water spring on top of a hill, all on his land. He's able to drink clean water and bathe whenever he desires.

His son buys all types of seeds to plant and grow for food and grass. He digs a path all through the land so he can water the crops and grass. Now the family can eat and sell food crops. He also sells water to the village people to drink. His son buys male and female animals to breed so they can have farm animals to eat as well as sell the meat. He uses the manure of his animals to help grow the crops better and sell them as well. The family got better with time, but it all started with a man who owned his own land and water spring...

Peace, Brother Vee,

One Love
Chase/Sabur
Keyon Sprinkle

L.I.F.E.

Life ain't always fair and there is no fairness within these man-made laws, especially for people of color! I'm living proof of it. Unjust law is no law at all. I can say I'm blessed and cursed in the same sentence because I learned really quickly not to accept or believe this "life- bid" was or is my final stop in this lifetime. Therefore, I refuse to give up on my fight for my physical freedom, my mother, my seeds and my true friends that support my cause. But most important, I refuse to give up on myself because if I do that they win. I'm a firm believer that all things happen for a real reason. So, I take heed to my trials and tribulations in life so that I can learn and grow from them. If I wasn't in prison today where I'm becoming a better man, I would still be lost (mentally). I would still be lost within my own darkness. I came to the light (truth) of self and it did not happen overnight, nor was it easy to accomplish. But I had a strong desire to change my life.

I went through the struggles of going to war with my lower self and earthly desires. We will always have struggles come our way, but we will know how to deal with them better when we have a higher understanding of our self and our situation. I can only speak for myself but I'm sure many can relate and respect the sincerity. I commend anyone who's willing to change for the better and grow as a person because this is not a game and these people are playing for keeps. If the youths only knew the world they are about to enter (prison) by risking their freedom, they would think twice about the choices they make out there in those streets.

I know many of us deal with the drama of our seeds' (kids) mothers when it comes to seeing our seeds so I can relate but always remember your seeds are you (smile). That's one thing their mother can never keep from you. Whoever is striving to be a father to their kids regardless of the situation, it's all about breaking that cycle we were born into. Within the confinement of these cold walls with nothing but my own thoughts bouncing off this hard metal,

I find myself with constant questions about him (my son). Those thoughts become my true lullaby. Does he look like me? Would he learn to love me if given the chance? Does he feel a void from my absence in his life? Will I ever get to touch his flesh and tell him that I love him? Days and days pass like hands on a clock, so fast when you stop paying attention, but so slow when you are. Some men in prison only think of their seed sixty percent of the time. My son is on my mind as if he is my source of existence because it is so easy to give up hope in this hell, I live every day.

While I'm in here I would still like to think I have something to offer my son and his precious soul. From the outside looking in things may look different, scary even, and it is. But behind these steel bars is a man aching for a chance to know and give all he has left to offer right now to this child with his DNA. Everything else has been stripped away. Yet my main concern is to do for this important addition to my heart. Some say I don't deserve a chance and to them I say, "Doesn't my son deserve a chance to decide?" Others may feel if I cared so much, I shouldn't have put myself in this predicament. To them I say, "Regardless of what happened, or whose fault it is, it has already happened. It is a matter which is done, and we must progress to the next chapter where we all want better for ourselves." People may say, "Why subject a child to such a negative atmosphere and circumstances?" My answer to them is, "My current circumstances does not alleviate the fact that my blood will course through his veins until he has none left. The way my eyes perceive things, I have the ability to offer him a truthful example of a place he doesn't want to enter."

It's a perspective beyond common sense, but one of experience and truth. Anyone can tell him I'm a loser who threw my life away and I'm worth nothing. They're entitled to their opinion but that is only one side of the story. Not one of those open mouths, spewing their opinions can offer these words: "You're not his father." I may not be equipped at this moment to provide him with the consistent camaraderie and emotional support which he deserves, but I'm offering all that I'm capable of giving; it counts for a lot in my eyes. No wall can ever prevent me from being a man!

Vee, I know you can feel my pain and my struggle. Thank you for allowing me to grace your book with my heart. Stay righteous, brother.

Sincerely,

Allen An war Alston

WHEN YOU'VE GOT A GOOD WOMAN TREAT HER RIGHT

My Queen,

I love you so much. You've stuck by my side through thick and thin and the toughest times. Thank you, baby. I am forever loyal to you. Queen, you witnessed me out there in those streets. I was so far gone, and I was in way too deep. I did not see the fall coming upon me. You were right there by my side through it all, whether I was right or wrong, you never left my side. Do you remember how we used to cruise the highways listening to our favorite Tupac songs? When I got locked up it was extremely hard on you, Queen. Our little lady was just two months old. Do you remember the first time you brought her to visit me and I just sat there crying while looking at her? That moment hurt so fucking bad. I had to blow the both of you kisses from behind that thick glass and you just shook your head as if asking me, "Why?"

Those first five years upstate were tough as a motherfucker. You left me and moved on with your life and I almost went crazy (smile). I couldn't understand how deep your pain was and I hated you for leaving me. But in reality, it was me who left you and our baby in a cold world all alone. I couldn't see the truth because I was so mentally deaf, dumb and blind at that time. But look at us now, Queen. We still go through our love, hell, right but overall, we're at peace with each other and the love is strong. Remember I used to tell you, "After the rain comes the sunshine."

It's been five years since we put our love back on track. We have not looked back since that special moment in the visiting room. Do you see how our baby's face lights up when we are giving her all of our attention? What about when she catches us giving each other small kisses?

Do you see how happy she gets? It's so amazing, baby. This journey has been so long, and I almost lost you once. But now we're almost at the finish line and we'll be together as a family again. Baby, you always tell me that you love me, and I know you do. I love you, too. That's why I have changed my life so I can come home and be the man I need to be for you and our child. We've traveled down a very long road together. It wasn't always smooth, but our strong bond and pure love carried us through... I love you, Queen.

Your husband,

Davon McNeil

SHE IS SO DAMN FILTHY

Check it out little homie, I was just like you. I was lost within that cold world, truly believing in the hood rules and the codes of the streets. My dude, you're not alone. Trust me, I'm feeling the same pain you're experiencing right now. You feel betrayed, right? It was all a lie, little homie! Just like you I went hard out there in those streets. I gave my whole life to that street shit, literally. The older dudes told you to keep it real and never talk to the police, right? Yeah, I was told the same shit, my dude. Didn't it hurt like a motherfucker when you realized that you were the only one playing by them bullshit rules? Shit, I still get heated when I think about that lame shit...real talk, homie. I was dumping whole clips, my G, all for the love of the hood.

Jail? Prison? Homie, I was in and out of County on the regular. My dude, what about this one? You got a bail and the hood make all kinds of excuses as to why they can't get the paper to bail you out. What about this one? When someone from your hood is on their way to get you but somehow never got there? I'm telling you homie; I feel your pain. I've been there. Now we are forced to cop out because if we go to trial the courts are going to slay us. Our records are crazy. So, we man-up and take the bid. It's nothing. Unfortunately, we know how to bid real well. Wait a minute, my G, where's the team? I thought they told us it was all about loyalty. What happened to "real Niggas to the end?" Why the fuck we ain't making canteen, homie? No flicks from the hood, my dude? Damn, my G, what the fuck is going on? You do remember they told us death before dishonor, right? Okay, fuck it. We just gonna rob everybody when we hit the bricks. Tell me that's not how you feel or felt, my G? I know the feeling very well. Every once in a while, your right-hand man may show you some love and send a few dollars your way; just enough to say he held you down, right? I'm telling you; it was all a lie and these Nigga's fake as fuck. All right let's forget all that fake shit. It is what it is.

Why is wifey the cause of all our major stress? She's here for a few good months and then she's in the wind, right homie? We're the happiest thugs in the whole prison when they call our name for a visit, right? Don't front, my dude. You were dressed two hours before they even called your name, huh? Yeah, I know what it's about, real talk. Then there're those days when you call wifey and can't even reach her. We calling back-to-back for like an hour straight, right? After about six hours had passed, she finally answers the phone and got a shitty attitude like you did something wrong, right? My dude, you couldn't reach her all fucking day and she got an attitude with you. Imagine that shit.

Homie check the fly-shit out though. So, you call your big Sis because it's been a while since you

checked in with the family. Big Sis is from the hood so she's putting you up on all the hood reports who got locked, who got shot, who got robbed and who dropped the latest V; you know how big Sis gets all extra-animated with that gossip shit (smile). Then out of the clear blue she asks you, "Bro," when was the last time you spoke to your wifey?"
Automatically you gotta take a shit and your hands get all sweaty because you already know Sis is about to drop some bullshit on you. Her next words are, "Yo bro, I don't want you in there stressing and shit, but I heard your wifey is out here fucking Victor (your right-hand man)." Homie, all you see is black, right? I swear, just sitting here thinking back on that foul shit, "it hurts, my dude" ...Trust me.

I been there. Now, with all that you just read, why are you still fucking with them streets? Tell me something, homie, do you enjoy the pain? I'm asking you a serious question, my dude. I've been in prison for the last ten years straight and this shit is fucking whack.

I'm 33 years old and I've been through many trials and tribulations. I have a family who loves me, and I have two beautiful daughters who I left to be raised by single mothers in that cold world. Do you want to know what my wife goes through raising my daughter on her own? You can't even imagine, homie. What about my mom who is out in the world with both of her legs missing due to diabetes, and two of her three sons locked up for murder? C'mon, my dude.

When do we finally say, "Enough is enough," and realize it was all a lie? That thing we called "the game" is honestly not a game at all. When we got sentenced to all this fucking time, the judge was not playing. So where is the game in that? All of the above are actual facts and were caused by my own hands. Let's start activating off of righteous thoughts, my people. Life is for the living! Love yourself first and get out of them streets.

Peace, Vee (Davon McNeil)

SCRIPTURE

"If I had ignored my sins the Lord would not have listened to me" (Psalms 66:18). To God be the glory because if it wasn't for the grace of God, I would be forever dead. Life, it's a time for awakening, a moment, the opportunity to produce and manifest, the essence of a seed planted. I have learned that, in order for there to be life, first there must be growth. Anything which is stagnant is considered dead; no longer producing. When those we call O.G.'s spit game to me in my youth, it was never to bring about my own identity, nor groom me into becoming my unique self. I was shown and encouraged to go out into the streets and get that money; take no shorts, keep it real and hold my own. However, I was never told about or shown the other side of the game; the part where during my first 12 years of living that wild illusion and shooting my gun for the hood, those same fellas would turn their backs on me while trooping this long ass bid. I got no visits, no mail, no money, no nothing. These were my so-called team members.

We took a silent oath to hold each other down no matter what. My son, Dayshawn, got no sneakers for school and my daughter, Love, got no school supplies.

I pledged my allegiance to a crew, and later a nation, whose belief and culture I no longer subscribe to. I gave my all to that culture which gave me nothing but a life of heartache and pain. Today, I have life-long enemies because of a way of life based on ignorance and lies.

Look at what I've caused my elderly mother to be subjected to: She has to have her bra removed to visit her son who caused her nothing but pure hell. And she's still going through hell having to deal with these wicked CO's. She has to be pat-searched and then walk through a damn metal detector. My kids must remove their shoes and the babies must have their diapers searched. My wife has left me because the pressure became too much for her to stand up under. Do I blame her or myself for putting her in that situation? Word got back from the street that she's now in a relationship with an enemy of mine.

I've allowed my loyalty to be my own downfall. Now I'm forced to share a cell with another grown ass man. We're both within a cage, striving to conceal our rage. No one could've ever told me that the same dudes I was brainwashed to hate, and kill would become some of the realest individuals I would ever meet. The same dudes that I had onsite drama within the streets are the same ones who would give up a bar of soap or a three-way call so I could talk to my mom or kids. I got family members who wouldn't do that for me. I've been betrayed by my own brothers and sisters. Listen, I don't want to keep you for too long, so just let me say these parting words: Keep the focus on yourself and become better than you already are. Know that you are great!

Peace and blessings,

Tyson

THIS IS HOW I SEE IT

I learned quickly that in the game of life what's really important is how quickly you can recover from hitting the deck, especially getting hit with one of life's stinging and crushing blows: a life bid! When I walked through the door with mine, I was sick and I didn't want to get better. So, I hung out with other sick cats. Some were sicker than me. I never thought that I would get better because I simply didn't want to. Then someone who was healing from his sickness told me the fight was not over. The referee was still counting. I could get up and fight to win.

First, you must start recovering. Affirm who you are to check your sanity. Shake the pain. Get your chin down and your guard up and keep moving forward. That's what I did. I wasn't fighting for the crowd, the accolades or the false pride. I was now fighting for my life. Every move I made from that point on was done with thought and principle. If it didn't coincide with me getting better and winning the bout then it was a no-brainer, I simply wouldn't do it.

ONE OF MY MOM'S OLD JAMS

It's hard times now. Just one crack at life. Who wants to live it in trouble and strife. My mind must be free to learn all I can about me. I'm gonna love me for the rest of my days. Encourage the babies every time they say "self-preservation is what's going on today.

-Candy Strayton-

No doubt always be true to yourself and to those who are true to you. It gets hard at times, we fall short, but practice does help. To make it back to the free world from a life sentence you need a focused mind, a real good lawyer and sometimes both. However, neither can be accomplished if you are not true to yourself. I speak from experience because I got off the deck twice and came back to win two giant decisions because I chose to recover and heal. You can't stew in misery and isolation with a life sentence because you'll remain your own worst enemy. So, live your life and find ways to become better than you were yesterday. Make friends and enrich your life while you still have one.

Muhammad Ali's greatest gift is that he always remained interesting. The only man who has more books written about him is Jesus. One thing is for sure, life is not fair or perfect, but you don't have to stay in prison for life unless you want to. Blaming others and certain situations which were caused by your own hands is sucker shit. Being a champ is not just about how well you execute your shots, but how you can take those same shots, absorb them, recover and stay on your own two feet.

Mr. Kurry Harbor

THE BARS WERE MADE TO HOLD Y'ALL...

I was made to hold y'all from your wifey and children and road dogs;
I'm a fucked-up building with cold bars.
My plans are to make your stay hard;
I love when you cry at your class boards.
Hearing your lies at parole boards; begging and pleading.

You're amped up when I let your family in once a weekend.
I see you when you sneak your weed in.
Oh you're a tough guy, yet through the crack of your cell door you whine;
Every night you realize I'm making you guys into real guys.

I get you stressed and make you kill guys, easily.
When you go home remember me.
I make females see your jail shine; they wanna fuck you because of me.
I never let those females touch you, Ha-ha!

Once my door shake, don't worry just rise and wake.
I'm temporary for you tough guys with brains, but for tough guys my road brings pain.
Hopefully you stay blind and do crime, cuz I was only built to do time.

Yo! Let me tell you about my workers. They stay mad.
Also, they can fuck with you on purpose.
Nobody is happy on the surface and the worse shit is when you get mad and wanna bum shit, leaving me scarred. I don't deserve it.
Your family long gone. They left you hurting. Me and my gates, you think we worthless.

Meeting your fate behind my curtains for selling them drugs and thug purpin.
Holding them guns illegally you never purchased. I'll finish you off and that's for certain.
You block kids think you cold and real hard. I never liked you.
I made you steal on guards and break white dudes.

In my system you get the worst move; seeing you in DDU is just a present to a thug from me to you.
I'm fucking up your visits. For six months they won't crack your biscuits.
You hear about your wifey dick-licking. She never liked you cuz she been tricking.
Yet you blame me, cuz you was on the bricks bullshitting. Yeah, right!

Once my door shake, don't worry just rise and wake.
I'm temporary for you tough guys with brains, but for tough guys my road brings pain.
Hopefully you stay blind and do crime, cuz I was only built to do time.

Why don't you check this, one table, two lockers, a trash can and a toilet to shit. I'm a nightmare for a guy with a kid.
My whole objective is for breaking you in;
Virgin thugs don't wanna face me again.

They getting bagged with drugs, but yet and still they never taste me again.
I take that personal; a prisonly sin.
Someone end up hurting you.
You should be glad when you come through.

I tripled the price on dope bags, weed and plus your coke, too.
Cripples and whites, I break you, too.
Niggaz and dykes, I don't discriminate.
To the Willies with ice, I never playa hate; DOC affiliate.

Controlled movement I own you.
And to thugs, I was built to hold you.
Motherfuckers, I'm prison!

Juice, One Love

ME AGAINST YOU

As Salaam Great Mind,

You already know, family...man brings about his own fate. Therefore, I welcome each day as it comes and greet it as it goes! No question this battle is real and the journey long and tiresome, so I stay with my knees bent and mind-frame militant. With this war comes great losses. For the weak, the price of loss can be your damn mind. This is some real mental torture on our loved ones. So if they can't handle it we strive to understand and not let that break us or our spirit. Do the knowledge, Great Mind. This prison thing is designed to break everyone's spirit and destroy your resolve. To do this, the authorities attempt to exploit every weakness, demolish every positive, negate all signs of individuality, all with the ideal of stomping out that magnetic spark which makes us stand strong and perpendicular on our square, thus showing and proving we are the original man! "We must never lighten up and always tighten up." Walls, chains and fences can't stop real progress if it's truly real. It only enhances our strategy.

I've been in prison 20 years and I'm still determined to take my free-dom back! I've never just settled for anything in my entire life so, of course, I'm not going to take this short either. Because of knowledge of self and many years of doing shit the wrong way, I was constantly serving myself justice. I knew better but was not doing better. However, my life is relevant today. I know and understand that my current situation is not a dream or nightmare. This shit is hell on earth. The owner of this modem day slave plantation gets a percentage off of my head just for being within his prison house. Dig that shit!

Great mind, a brother gotta come into this motherfucker on day one, hitting the law library and becoming intimate with his case. Because this prison is no joke and these devils got three shifts which they rotate so they'll never get tired, ya dig! We must go at this thing as if our life really depends on it, because it does. These motherfuckers are playing for keeps. This is not checkers but chess, family. Every move sets up your next move: Rule 30, then direct appeal. However, without knowledge of this thinking man's game, a brother will serve every day of that life bid!

Let's wake up black people and learn. We can't keep being too strong in all the wrong areas. We gotta start acting like we know what's going on around us. This shit is live rounds and a motherfucker can literally die in this bitch if brothers don't get for real with their self and these life bids. Fuck that slick talk and a visit. The law library holds all the keys to our freedom!

Come with it, Family!

(Shareef)

Peace, Victory

FOOD FOR THOUGHT

As Salam Walaikum
Surah 4:79

      (Inshallah) You do the dishes!

In the Holy Qur'an God states, "Whatever good (O, man), happens to thee is, from Allah, but whatever evil happens to thee is from thy (own) soul"...so as I evaluate my life as a whole and my current situation, I can only ponder and reflect on the errors and misguidedness of my ways. The understanding I had which dictated my thoughts, ways and actions was from the minds of other men, not my own. Also, family, neighborhood, music, society and friends played a major part in my life. So how am I to be counterculture to the negativity which governed my understanding or way of life?

In the Holy Qur'an God states, "Allah will never change the condition of a people until they change what is in their own soul (Surah 8:53)... My mind has been dictated by the words of God, not the words of other men. In order to change the condition of my soul I must examine and evaluate myself. Now the Arabic word for "soul" has a much broader meaning in its translation. I had to examine and change the condition of my bad habits, my psychology and the things which were hereditary; the effects of my background, my schooling, my hidden and repressed feelings; and lastly, my attitude. It is only when embarking on this journey of repairing, refocusing and regrouping that I can begin to tap into the master builder of self which was created by God in the womb. How so?

In the Holy Qur'an God states, "By the soul and the proportion, and an order given to it, and its enlightenment as to its wrong and its right, truly he succeeds that purifies it and he fails that corrupts it!" God makes the soul and gives it order, proportion and relative perfection in order to adapt it for the particular circumstances in which it has to live its life. He breathes into it an understanding of what is sin, impiety and wrongdoing, what is piety and right conduct. This is the most precious gift to all man: the faculty to distinguish between right and wrong. By this very token man should learn that his success, prosperity and his salvation depends on him; on his keeping his soul pure as Allah made it. Also, his failure, his decline and his perdition depends on his soiling by choosing evil, negativity, wrongdoing, etc.

In conclusion, I want to salute all the lifers I've encountered on my journey of rebuilding. They have left a permanent impression of inspiration because they've gotten their bodies trapped by their own hands. However, by those same hands they've allowed their minds to be set free, and most importantly, they remain relevant. With that being said. I'll end the way I began:

As Salam Walaikum

Dawud Salahuddin Ali

Vee stay infinite.
Peace my people!

P.S. "Know the consequences of your actions and you'll always make the right decision!"

IN THE NAME OF ALLAH AND JUSTICE

Peace Universe,

Prison is harder in more ways than I can spill in a letter with the politics and constant bombardment of bullshit coming at you from all four corners. It's a mental and physical war with other prisoners, C.O.'s and the administration. And the greatest of those opponents is the war with "self." Without self-determination, sponsorship and support, a man's mentality becomes warped in prison.

"Oppression begets violence because oppression is itself, an act of violence."
                                                                                Franz Fanon

It is extremely difficult for men to maintain their sanity in an oppressive environment which keeps its prisoners far removed from societal progression and social norms. We don't have real connections to our communities and families. And the absence (or strained rapport with such because of DOC policies) of our communities and/or families under these conditions make rehabilitation and successful re-entry back into our communities and our homes absolutely impossible!

These prison institutions aren't breeding productive citizens. The environment is too oppressive. In essence, it's violent at both the mental and physical levels. The DOC policies suppress rather than encourage the real growth of the prisoner here in Massachusetts so staying self-determined in here is my struggle. But I will beat the odds. Those of you who have family, friends and loved ones in the system, your support and sponsorship makes the difference and can create the greats of society as opposed to the DOC who is only creating the menace...and so, "With love stands by those who want better."

Supreme 7 Allah
One of the great minds
Within the devil's oppressive compounds!
Peace to the righteous.

MY YOUTH GONE!

Damn, a life bid at 15 years old. I know you're probably saying to yourself, "He's just a baby. He didn't know any better." But that's not what this white man's world calls it nor do they see it that way. To them I'm a murderer; a stone-cold killer; a savage; a no-good lowlife. That's what I am to these people. However, I don't see myself in this light. To me, I was a lost soul striving to be like everyone else (my peers) around me who had a huge influence on my way of thinking. I saw the older dudes selling drugs in order to buy nice clothing so they could attract the females in our neighborhood. I wanted the same thing, so I followed in their footsteps. But look at me know.

I'm doing a natural life sentence in prison. All those material things I was living for and the women I wanted, where is it and where are they now? I'm all alone doing this time. Where are my so-called boys? I thought y'all were going to ride with me to the end? I guess this life bid is the end, huh? Where are all the pretty young ladies who were so-called in love with me? That's right. They're no longer in sight. Like the saying goes, "Out of sight out of mind." I'm like a memory to them now. But why is that? I'm not physically dead. I'm still alive and breathing. I'm just held in a cell; a cold cage like I'm some kind of animal. Where is all the love and loyalty I was promised?

I remember when I was free and always wanting to be in the streets with my boys, hanging out. My grandmother used to say, "Baby, those are not your friends. Stop hanging with them because you're going to find yourself in trouble." But all that wisdom she was giving me was going into one ear and out the other. Now, because I chose not to listen to the people who truly loved me, I'm sitting within a place where we're considered the walking dead. Damn, it sucks being in here all alone. But please don't get these written words twisted because I know this is not the last stop for me. I know I'm going home one day through the grace of the Almighty God. Yeah, I know that He has a plan for me. I just don't know when that plan will come.

Before I end this message, I just want to say to whoever is reading this, love yourself before you love anyone else. Know who you are and believe in yourself. Take advice from the people who love you because they've been through the same trials and tribulations and have made the same mistakes. They're telling you these things because they love you. Please listen to your love ones. I didn't listen to mine and now I'm sitting in prison doing a natural life bid...Take care and God bless.

Vee, you're a good brother. Keep doing what you're doing to enlighten our youths. Thanks for sharing space in your book with me.

Peace,

Truly, Short

WE WILL MAKE IT

A closed mouth don't get fed! Men who are self-aware and grounded in knowledge not only stand on their foundations but "produce" their "realities." Knowledge without execution is equivalent to "prayer without deeds." Many men know better but because "they lack vision" and the ability to breed unity, nothing more than an island is produced which they themselves are stranded on. A basic simple truth: "No man is an island." But all of us can't just open our mouths to be heard. We must create a momentum in the earth which will shake governments. After all, it's an elevated sound, Black Man. Aren't we created to carry or pitch that? Person=per=Latin for "through" and Sona=sound, both meaning "a person is something through which sounds travel."

True, scientists agree that our personalities are "vibrations" and expressions, but not the ears of self. This is why we're constantly turning down falsehoods to get closer to the truth because when we find that, we find ourselves. Men who understand conquer within that union—it's like all truths—it represents itself. Therefore, I never listen to what men say. It's what they produce that speaks their truth. Are they producing freedom, justice and equality for themselves or for their people? Are they producing more educators and warriors to the cause or advancement? When our people are weak-minded, weak-spirited and non-productive brothers, they're a reflection of us! Just as our excellence is an example for them.

Our ability and discipline to overcome great obstacles serves as an example for them. This is why history rewards its researcher. Am I speaking in tongues or theory? No! We bear witness that in this two-year span, 2008 - 2010, we have made history with the Governor's visit to look at the black man's condition at this prison house. We had the Commissioner, Harold Clark, come address our African Heritage Coalition Group to deal with the culture clash at O.C.C.C. It was a clash because black men refused to be intimidated or abused. It was black intelligence which reigned supreme to create those victories. We remained while the administration crumbled around us. But the average eye cannot see or mentally understand they themselves are the original authors of life and lost warriors. There is no idea too big for the black mind to hold or achieve! We are living truths of this reality. True wisdom produces its reality to upset falsehoods. So, when men rely on excuses rather than their wisdom, they have no idea of the real concept, but have learned to sound intelligent instead of living intelligently...

Peace and love to the future.
Master self (1) and the world will open to your dreams.
4+5=9 4x90=360 3+6+0=9 4+2+3=9

Mack Hudson, M- 11

REMEMBERING THE PAST

There is much to be gained by remembering and learning from the past. There is also much to be gained by remembering that the past does not need to control you. Now is the time to build. Now is where you are. Now is when you are fully alive; fully able to make things happen. Wishing things had been different steals energy away from the positive action you can take right now because now, instead of merely wishing, you can act now to make it happen. All the disappointments you've ever experienced are now behind you. Though these consequences may continue, those disappointments no longer hold you back. In fact, now in this moment, you have the power to turn each disappointment completely around. You can, with your thoughts and actions, redirect your energy in whatever direction you choose. When you break free of the chains which hold your thinking in the past, you'll discover something truly amazing: All that is now is much, much more than enough.

Peace,
The Convict

WHY ARE YOU SO MAD?

Anger is an unstable state of emotion. When angry, people are prone to act irrationally. When acting irrationally people are apt to make mistakes. These mistakes can be detrimental to those who make them and beneficial to those who exploit them. Therefore, anger is a weakness and those who allow themselves to be manipulated by it are easily defeated. Always do the knowledge to people, places and things. Never allow your emotions to rule you because you're at their mercy. Stay in tune with your true self: your true mind. It's always knowledge before wisdom. Understanding is the best part. Positive education always corrects errors. We will never be truly free until we take the shackles off of our minds!

Pure Vision,

Peace.

WE'VE BEEN LIED TO

Damn, O.G., why you do me like this? All you kept telling me was that I was a thorough young Nigga with a lot of potential. I looked up to you, O.G. I remember seeing you in front of the crack spot in '89. That's something I'll never forget. You had on the black Champion with the pointed hood, black, silver-tabbed Levi's, all black Top Ten's and the black leather waistcoat from Wilson's. You called me over to you and asked me why I was out there so late. My response was, "Dog, I'm just trying to finish this five-pack." You smiled that crooked smile of yours and told me to take a walk with you. You gave me the rules of "the game" first-hand and told me there's three rules I must live by no matter what: (1) to hustle hard and save everything, (2) stay loyal to the game and I would be alright, and (3) most importantly, never talk to the police about anything.

Walking with you that night was one of the happiest and best moments of my life (so I thought at the time). The feeling was wonderful. I was walking with a certified hood star. We ended up at crack-head Stacy's house where you kept your dog, Scarface. I remember Stacy asking me how old I was. When I told her, I was 12 years old, she looked at you and said, "What the hell you doing with this baby out in the streets at 12 o'clock at night?" All you did was smile that crooked smile and you told her I was your little homie and she would see my face in the hood more often, so look out for me. I remember you asked me if I smoked weed and I said, "A little bit." I had only smoked twice before, and I don't think I did it right; smoking with you had me laughing at all types of shit.

We ate two boxes of cereal back-to-back (Stacy's kids' cereal) and I remember your dog kept barking every time someone knocked at the door. You'd tell the dog to relax because it was only money at the door. I remember you pulled out knots of money from all your pockets (a lot of money) and started counting it. I remember you laid out all the bills, facing them in the same direction (a habit which stayed with me my whole life). You told me to stay at Stacy's house and told her to help me finish my pack. You gave her a 50-block and told her to make sure I was straight. You called a Yellow Cab and told Scarface to get ready. The dog walked over to a corner and grabbed his leash (my love for Pits began that night). I remember you looked at me and said, "Little homie, you next in line."

If I could go back to that night in '89 I would have never taken that walk with you, O.G. I'm sitting in Old Colony Correctional Center, serving a life bid because of that walk 19 years ago. There's so much which you neglected to tell me about that thing called "the game." I went through so much shit out there in those streets just because you said, "I had potential." When you looked at me in

Stacy's house that night in '89 and said I was next in line, O.G., you were not bullshitting. On ice cream day or a hot summer's day in this prison yard these lines are long as hell... (Smile).

Damn, O.G., why you do me like that?

"Vee" (Davon McNeil)

LIVE A LIFE THAT MATTERS

Ready or not, someday it will all come to an end. There will be no more sunrises, no minutes, hours or days. All things you've collected, whether treasured or forgotten will pass to someone else. Your wealth, fame and temporal power will shrivel to irrelevance. It will not matter what you owned or what you were owed. Your grudges, resentments, frustrations and jealousies will finally disappear. So, too, does your hopes, ambitions, plans and to-do lists will expire. The wins and losses which once seemed so important will fade away. In the end, it won't matter where you came from or on what side of the tracks you lived. It won't even matter whether you were beautiful or brilliant. Even your gender and skin color will be irrelevant.

So, what will matter? How will the value of your days be measured? What will matter is not what you bought, but what you have built; not what you got, but what you gave. What will matter is not your success, but your significance. What will matter is not what you have learned, but what you taught. What will matter is every act of integrity, compassion, courage or sacrifice which enriched, empowered or encouraged others to emulate your example. What will matter is not your competence, but your character. What will matter is not how many people you knew, but how many will feel a lasting loss when you're gone. What will matter are not your memories, but the memories which live in those who love you. What will matter is how long you will be remembered and by whom and for what. Living a life that matters doesn't happen by accident. It's not a matter of circumstance, but of choice. Choose to live a life that matters.

The Mystery Author!

EVERYTHING!!!

What's good, family? And I say family because I believe we are all connected through interdependence. Basically, we all play a role in society and life which is directly connected to one another. For instance, I'm a drug-addicted criminal. So I employ doctors and police. And I got no love for the jakes (police). What I really want to talk about is something else. Like most people from a broken home I was forced to become a man before my time. My dad was absent, so I learned to be a man on my own (at least what I thought was a man). While some of my perception was clearly common sense, my integrity was clouded and therefore was compromised out of the gate. Nobody was to blame. I formed my own opinions and morals based upon my surroundings. My idea of a man was that of a breadwinner, strong, respected, feared, ruthless, loyal, honest and powerful; the one with the biggest gun and most money commanded all of the above. But a man was never to be soft, caring, kind, loving or anything of that nature. Emotions were a sign of weakness.

Over the years I've learned my ways could be wrong, not because someone forced change down my throat, but because it felt wrong. I lived my way and got pain, strife and loss. Then I awoke one day with clear eyes. I maintained all my positive attributes and worked on what I considered my defects, one at a time. Over a period of time I noticed a change in my life as well as my circle of loved ones. I became more satisfied with life. I was able to express emotions without feelings of shame. I was earning the respect of real men; good men. See, you can be a man anyway you look at it. But there are only two kinds of men: good and bad. It's okay to care for a woman and say you love her. It's okay to have your feelings hurt. It's how you deal with it which shapes your character.

I heard someone say, "You are who you want to be, and if you work hard with integrity and conviction you can reach any goal you set for yourself." Throughout your journey you never need to change your morals. I am who I want to be. I work on my inner self every day. Who I want to be is very simple: just me. I just want to be a better man — to my family. I never fear change. I was given an acronym by a very wise young man who told me that FEAR is only False Energy Appearing Real!

Rocky

THE COMMUNITY OF BROTHERS

My community of brothers, when you look within the mirror "know" that you are "great." Never allow yourself to be defined by mistakes.

Let's extend hands to each other.
And desire to recover.

You are not your addiction.
You are pure benediction (a blessing).

Our community is only what we make it.
Let's draw strength from each other and not allow our monsters to take it.

When you are feeling low, speak about it and let someone know.
Brother, if you're low the community can't grow.

Our lives have meaning, and we're created for a divine purpose.
Please brothers, do not ever believe that you are worthless.

We all have the power to avoid our triggers.
Our "will" to recover just needs to be bigger.

Trust the truth, think it through, step slow and steady.
We're a strong community. Help, strength, trust and

respect is here whenever you are ready.

We're a community!

Graduate Mentor, Davon M.

Davon McNeil

THE SECRET TEACHING THAT CHANGED RAP

Hello,

After more than 20 years I've finally decided to tell the world what I witnessed in 1991, which I believe was one of the biggest turning points in popular music, and ultimately American society. I have struggled for a long time, weighing the pros and cons of making this story public, because I was reluctant to implicate the individuals present that day. So, I've simply decided to leave out names and all the details which might risk my personal well-being and that of those who were, like me, dragged into something they were not ready for.

Between the late '80s and early '90s I was what you might call a "decision maker" with one of the more established companies in the music industry. I came from Europe in the early '80s and quickly established myself in the business. The industry was different back then. Since technology and media weren't accessible to people like they are today, the industry had more control over the public and had the means to influence them anyway it wanted. This might explain why in early 1991, I was invited to attend a closed-door meeting with a small group of music insiders to discuss rap music's new direction. Little did I know we would be asked to participate in one of the most unethical and destructive business practices I've ever seen.

The meeting was held at a private residence on the outskirts of Los Angeles. I remember about 25 to 30 people being there, most of them familiar faces. Speaking to those I knew, we joked about the theme of the meeting as many of us did not care for rap music and failed to see the purpose of being invited to a private gathering to discuss its future. Among the attendees was a small group of unfamiliar faces who stayed to themselves and made no attempt to socialize beyond their circle. Based upon their behavior and formal appearances, they didn't seem to be in our industry.

Our casual chatter was interrupted when we were asked to sign a confidentiality agreement preventing us from publicly discussing the information presented during the meeting. Needless to say, this intrigued, and in some cases disturbed, many of us. The agreement was only a page in length but very clear on the matter and consequences which stated that violating the terms would result in job termination. We asked several people what this meeting was about and the reason for such secrecy but couldn't find anyone who had answers for us. A few people refused to sign and walked out. No one stopped them. I was tempted to follow but curiosity got the best of me. A man who was part of the "unfamiliar" group collected the agreements from us.

Quickly after the meeting began one of my industry colleagues (who shall remain nameless like everyone else) thanked us for attending. He then gave the floor to a man who only introduced himself by his first name and gave no further details about his personal background. I think he was the owner of the residence, but it was never confirmed. He briefly praised all of us for the success we had achieved in our industry and congratulated us for being selected as part of this small group of "decision makers." At this point I began to feel slightly uncomfortable at the strangeness of the gathering. The subject quickly changed as the speaker went on to tell us that the respective companies, we represented had invested in a very profitable industry which could become even more rewarding with our active involvement. He explained that the companies we work for had invested millions into the building of privately-owned prisons. Our positions of influence in the music industry would actually impact the profitability of these investments.

I remember many of us in the group immediately looking at each other in confusion. At the time, I didn't know what a private prison was, and I was not the only one. Sure enough, someone asked what these prisons were and what any of this had to do with us. We were told that these prisons were built by privately-owned companies who received funding from the government based upon the number of inmates. The more inmates, the more money the government would pay these prisons. It was also made clear to us that since these prisons are privately-owned, as they became publicly traded, we'd be able to buy shares. Most of us were taken aback by this. Again, a couple of people asked what this had to do with us.

At this point my industry colleague who had first opened the meeting took the floor again and answered our questions. He told us that since our employers had become silent investors in this prison business, it was now in their interest to make sure that these prisons remained filled. Our job would be to make this happen by marketing music which promotes criminal behavior; rap being the music of choice. He assured us it would be a great situation for us because rap music was becoming an increasingly profitable market for our companies. As employers we would be able to buy personal stock in these prisons.

Immediately, silence came over the room. You could have heard a pin drop. I remember looking around to make sure I wasn't dreaming and saw half of the people with dropped jaws. My daze was interrupted when someone shouted, "Is this a f***** joke?" At this point things became chaotic. Two of the men who were part of the "unfamiliar" group grabbed the man who shouted out and attempted to remove him from the house. A few of us, myself included, tried to intervene. One of them pulled out a gun and we all backed off. They separated us from the crowd and all four of us were escorted outside. My industry colleague who had opened the meeting earlier hurried out to meet us and reminded us we had signed an agreement and would suffer consequences of speaking about this publicly or even with those who attended the meeting. I asked him why he was involved with something this corrupt. He told me it was bigger than the music business and nothing we'd want to challenge without risking consequences. We all protested and as he walked back into the house, I remember word-for- word the last thing he said: "It's out of my hands now. Remember you signed an agreement." Then he closed the door behind him.

The men rushed us to our cars and actually watched until we drove off. A million things were going through my mind as I drove away. I eventually decided to pull over and park on a side street in order to collect my thoughts. I replayed everything in my mind, repeatedly, which seemed very surreal to me. I was angry with myself for not taking a more active role in questioning what had been presented to us. I'd like to believe the shock of it all is what suspended my better nature. After what seemed like an eternity, I was able to calm myself enough to make it home.

The next day back at the office, I was visibly out of it but blamed it on being under the weather. No one else in my department had been invited to the meeting and I felt a sense of guilt for not being able to share what I had witnessed. I thought about contacting the three others who were kicked out of the house but didn't remember their names. Then I thought that tracking them down would probably bring unwanted attention. I considered speaking out publicly at the risk of losing my job but realized I'd probably be jeopardizing more than my job and I wasn't willing to risk anything happening to my family. I thought about those men with guns and wondered who they were. I had been told this was bigger than the music business and all I could do was let my imagination run free. There were no answers and no one to talk to. I tried to do a little bit of research on private prisons but didn't uncover anything about the music business' involvement. However, the information I did find confirmed how dangerous this prison business really was.

Days turned into weeks and weeks into months. Eventually, it was as if the meeting had never taken place. It all seemed surreal. I became more reclusive and stopped going to any industry events unless professionally obligated to do so. On two occasions, I found myself attending the same functions as my former colleague. Both times our eyes met but nothing more was exchanged. As the months passed, rap music had definitely changed direction. I was never a fan of it but even I could tell the difference. Rap acts which talked about politics or harmless fun were quickly fading away as gangster rap started dominating the airwaves. Only a few months had passed since the meeting, but I suspect the ideas presented that day had been fully implemented.

It was as if an order had been given to all major label executives. The music was climbing the charts and most companies were more than happy to capitalize on it. Each one was churning out their very own gangster rap acts on an assembly line. Everyone bought into it, consumers included. Violence and drug use became a central theme in most rap music. I spoke to a few of my peers in the industry to get their opinions on the new trend but was repeatedly told it was all about supply and demand. Sadly, many of them even expressed that the music reinforced their prejudice of minorities. I officially quit the music business in 1993 but my heart had already left months before. I broke ties with the majority of my peers and removed myself from this thing I once loved. I took some time off, returned to Europe for a few years, settled out of state and lived a "quiet" life away from the world of entertainment.

As the years passed, I managed to keep my secrets, fearful of sharing it with the wrong person but also a little ashamed of not having the balls to blow the whistle. But as rap got worse, my guilt grew. Fortunately, in the late '90s, having the internet as a resource which wasn't at my disposal in the early days, made it easier for me to investigate what is now labeled the prison industrial complex. Now that I have a greater understanding of how private prisons operate, things make much more sense than they ever have. I see how the criminalization of rap music played a big part in promoting racial stereotypes as well as misguided so many impressionable young minds into adopting these glorified criminal behaviors which often lead to incarceration.

Twenty years of guilt is a heavy load to carry. But the least I can do now is share my story, hoping that fans of rap music realize how they've been used for the past two decades. Although I plan to remain anonymous for obvious reasons, my goal now is to get this information out to as many people as possible. Please help me spread the word. Hopefully, others who attended the meeting back in 1991 will be inspired by this and tell their own stories. Most importantly, if only one life has been touched by my story, I pray it makes the weight of my guilt a little more tolerable.

Thank you.

THE GAME

What you call the game, I know it as pain.
How do we claim to truly love our children?
You don't feel ashamed?
You don't feel the pain?

You know your child is in the world all alone. No, daddy ain't coming home!
Your baby girl at her bus stop getting soaked in the rain.
Oh, I get it, you're in love with the game. To you it's a game!
You too tough for the pain...

Well, let me share something with you,
Something real I been through.
I watched my comrade cry. Yeah, he cried.
The Deacon brought the news to him. His mom just died.

Six years in on his natural life sentence.
Stop pretending! You laugh at the man while he up here speaking his truth.
Your fear got you stuck, wishing he was you.
I see your dry tears. I smell your fears. Let it go.
C'mon up here.

Addiction is mean.
I know dope fiends,
Who scratch their skin until it bleeds,
While nodding in their dreams.

How can you recover?
Get home to your sick mother?
You can't even sit still.
Cross-talking with your brother.

C'mon man, there are dudes in here who really want to recover from that thing you call the game.
We know it as pain. Stop playing with your life, it's not a game.
Wake up you sleeping giant. Unshackle the chain of addiction wrapped around your brain...
Stop crying inside, embrace your pain.

Your soul is on fire. Go ahead, jump into the flames.
Oh you scared now?
I thought you loved the game?
I feel your pain. It's not a game!

Davon M.

THROUGH THE FIRE

*Evil intentions have been erased by serenity,
Replaced by bliss incapable of explanation.
I fell into the gutter with ease through my extremities.
Though now, myself and those days no longer have relations.

*The memories linger through the pain which I avoid;
I fear as time goes on they may never be forgotten.
A constant reconstruction of a life that was destroyed;
After an epic battle with the wicked and the rotten.

*The fight goes on, for I found peace in a cemetery;
Caged in a village among the living dead.
I thank the Lord that my stay is only momentary;
A blessing disguised which I never will forget.

*1 feel that I have changed but I know that's not the case;
I have simply found myself after years of destruction.
It is a revelation that my salvation is this place;
For it has taken me away from the true hell I had been sucked into.

*It is impossible to say that each incident has no purpose;

While destiny is watching and fate is always lurking.
So I can't say that all my faults and falls were worthless;
Because I found strength, among the aching and hurting.

Through heaven and hell, divinity and disaster;
In search for wisdom to heal my desires.
Through pleasure and pain, tears and laughter;
Still I stand, I made it through the fire.

Christopher Webb

I FOUND IT...PEACE

Peace,

My aim is to give you, the reader, a glimpse into my reality. My name is Little Man aka Shine Poe. My honorable name, the name my mother blessed me with is Aderito Barbosa. I've spent the majority of my life in DYS facilities and prisons. For many, many years I never understood that my actions were a direct manifestation of my thoughts. Life to me had no meaning simply because my values were unconsciously skewed. My life was lived in the moment. My uncivilized way of living caused me to experience many trials and tribulations. Growing into adulthood while incarcerated has allowed me to recognize a great number of things which I could not see within my past life while in society; family being the most important thing. Family is something I took for granted and did not cherish due to my mentally blind state of existence. Today I fully understand the value of family and I have supreme appreciation for mine.

Now, for those who may not know me or my current situation, I was initially charged with first-degree murder. I was tried within a court of law and was ultimately acquitted of the murder charge but was found guilty of lesser charges and sentenced to 14 to 15 years in State prison. For the entire duration of my trial none of my so-called friends were there to support me. Every day through the rain, sleet and snow, my family was by my side, supporting me. That was a very humbling experience because I'd always put my so-called friends before my family. As I sat beside my lawyer in that huge courtroom, I thought to myself, "Where are all my friends who told me they would be there for me to the end? I guess me sitting here by myself in front of the judge was the end." Being able to recognize this harsh reality regarding my family and my so-called friends, I now realize I am fully and forever in debt to my family.

While sitting within many prison cells surrounded by cold steel and concrete, I had more than enough time to ponder on my life. The more I thought about my current situation, and the more information I was able to take into my mind and seriously meditate on it, the more life became clearer to me. Things started to make sense to me in a major way. There's a lesson in all things. We just have to see them. I am 100% sure had I not come to prison and spent the amount of time I did in solitary confinement (the hole), plus spent the time I did within DDU which allowed me to have plenty of alone time to reevaluate my thoughts, I would not be the man I am today. A life-change was warranted. I began to become more conscious of the thoughts I kept and what I allowed to come out of my mind. I also became aware of the company I kept around me. My decision-making became a lot wiser. Mentally as well as physically I began to experience true peace, which was foreign to me.

I've spent the last ten years of my life in prison and I've got four years left on my sentence. I'm not an individual who has lost my life to the system because as I sit here writing this message, I know many, many men who will never see the outside of these prison walls again. Many men I've met along my journey will die within prison. I've had the opportunity to sit with many men who will eventually die behind these prison walls. We've spoken on some really intense, heart-felt topics. Almost all of these great men have spoken the exact same words to me: "If only I knew then what I know now."

Please understand that life is not a game. Each time you allow negativity to become your guide, you're putting your life in the balance. There's nothing funny about, facing natural life in prison. I was there and I know exactly what it feels like to have your life flash before your eyes.

Prison has broken many great men in many unfortunate ways. I've seen men take their own life because of the pressure and stress prison life buried their souls under.

Peace!

HUMANITY IS YOUR TRUE SELF

Humanity is your true self. If you are outside of it, you will be attracted to other things. You will find yourself lost and enjoying it. You will be happy just to imitate life and not be real. This is the time we are living in.

Stay Wise!

THE SCIENCE TO INCREASE KNOWLEDGE

KNOWLEDGE - WISDOM - UNDERSTANDING
(Wisdom is the principle thing)
The beginning of knowledge is fear of the Lord.
What is the fear of the Lord?
To hate evil. Watching your tongue; pride removed.
Before honor is humility.
The Lord is just and righteous in all His ways.
Our will must be to do the will of Him, the Lord God.
Jesus is the light in darkness; "Follow."
Being born again, all things are made new.
By accepting Jesus Christ as our Lord and Savior.
Admitting we are sinners, asking for forgiveness
and by sinning no more we receive salvation
through the blood of Christ unto the day of
resurrection into eternal life; instead of resurrection
into eternal damnation.

(Wisdom being the principle thing)
The Lord said, "Let all ye ways be established."
Meaning, take the time to ponder the paths your
feet take.
For it was by knowledge, wisdom and
understanding that the Lord established the
heavens and the earth and gave the sea its decree
not to pass and engulf the earth.
Out of all of God's creations, man was given
dominion (RULE) over the birds of the air, the

creatures in the sea and the beasts on the earth.

They are all doing what the Lord intended them to do, EXCEPT MAN, for his will is of his own and not of his Father from which all things, all blessings and life come from.
Remember, Jesus is our example to follow and believe.
But we must surrender our will to do His will.
The Kingdom of GOD on earth is within the hearts of those who give their will over to do the will of God. Amen.

That's why I tell you these things.
(The beginning of knowledge)
Pray the Lord increase your understanding.
GOD BLESS. ONE LOVE.

Justin P. Douglas

P.S. The wisdom of man will be destroyed because there's another wisdom hidden from man until its appointed time. That is the knowledge of God. Peace...

PEACE, YOUNG QUEEN

Peace, Young Queen!

I love you, Juel. I was looking at a few of your pictures when you were a little younger and I knew then that I had me a star (smile).

Are you sticking to the plan and preparing yourself for a glorious future? Well, I am. Mentally, I'm ready to create heaven right here on earth.

Heaven to me is not somewhere all spooky and in space. It's right here on earth with my family and friends around me, having a wonderful time. Heaven for me is going to be teaching all of my family the TRUTH about their history (BLACK HISTORY).

Love is to be kept within a special place, behind a steel door.
Juel, never allow ANYONE to steal our love.
If you remain focused on your future and what you're going to create with your MIND, your LIFE will manifest the exact MENTAL picture.
Do you understand what I'm telling you?
I'm telling you that you're the sole controller of your destiny.
Eat right. Think right. Do right. Act right. Love right.

I love you so much!
Daddy

WHY?

Why did I have to be born into this world?
Before it was prison it was fast living.
But, I don't want to talk about the past. I want to talk about right here, now.
I stand before you today as a second-degree lifer...

I'm striving to recover from a lot of pain.

When I get up here and speak wisdom, do you really listen?
We're men trapped in prison.
How often do you reflect on your children?
If your son was drowning in a pool of water, gasping for air in front of your daughter, but she's only two years old;
Mommy, she can't call her.
What could you do to save your child?
When our community is said and done, we will go back to playing games, having fun.
You're not even going to think about your son.
I have two daughters and right now they're drowning in a pool of water...
What can I do to save them?
Where is their father?
I'm striving to recover from a lot of pain!

Peace to the CRA community!
Divine Victory Allah
Peace

MY PHILOSOPHY

First, let us know these things,
That our lives do matter.
I didn't want to be in them "streetz."
I was there cuz I had to be.
If I didn't trap, me and my little brothers didn't eat.
Yes, my family loves me and they need my love,
but tell that to them boyz around the corner who lay
in bushes, masks and gloves.

No, I am not a victim of circumstances.
My mother was an addict. My father was upstate,
so to the block I went, to take chances.

To stay free I had to master my habits.
So I invested in a big, black-matic; I slept in
hallways until the sun came up.
I've hardly seen my daughters.
It was money over everything.
I had to have it.

Look deep into my history and you'll see that my
people were held hostage, murdered because of
fear and anger.
Brought in chains to a wilderness, surrounded by
strangers.

Stripped of our identity, forced to love the very
creatures that did it to me. Pain, desperation and
thoughtless harm.

Through it all we remained strong. We will keep holding on.

But I will never forget nor will I ever just get over it. Bodies stacked on top of bodies. Blood, sweat, tears, feces, death and piss.

My history tells me the sharks trailed the ships. Atlantic Ocean. The valley of dry bones at the bottom of it.

That we can be part of something greater than ourselves, I will tell that truth to all of the young stars.

How can I be a great father from behind these prison bars?
She said, "Daddy, daddy please come home." I suffer from a broken heart. I'm mentally scarred.

Then let us do these things.
Humble ourselves to learning out of respect for our own potential. Study your history; It's very essential.

Listen, get knowledge, get wisdom and get a full understanding.
Now, let's sit down and build. Let's start doing some future planning.

Take courage against our fears and be steady in our efforts so that what is waiting within us can grow.

Let's get out of prison, raise our kids and teach them to become strong and beautiful.

Draw strength from each other. For the one who falls low, lock elbows with him.

Let's change our MENTALITY and stay out of prison.

Our thoughts will allow us to rise higher and higher.

I'm striving extremely hard to escape this mental fire!

And in all of this let us be guided by our highest power which is the MIND...

Love, honor, deserve and desire.
We're still doing time.

Thank you, "Allah the Father" ...
Davon McNeil, Divine (22) Allah
Peace!

I LOVE YOU, DADDY

Hi Daddy,

How are you doing? I hope you're alright and staying out of trouble. You always say that I don't write you, so I thought I would send you a short message. Daddy, I miss you so much. I really hope when you come home you never leave me again. Mommy told me that before I was born you left her, too. Is that true, Daddy? You always say I can ask you anything and you'll tell me the truth, so I want to ask you this. Daddy, "Do you really, really love me? Well, I'm 13 years old now and I need my father in my life. Is it true I was only two months old when you left me and mommy? The reason I'm asking you these questions is because I love you, Daddy. I want you to think about how I feel not having you in my life; here with me. I like talking to you on the phone but sometimes I be mad at you.

Mommy and I caught a flat tire the other day and she started crying on the side of the road. When I asked her what was wrong, she said she was tired of doing this by herself. A lady pulled over and helped us. I know you and mommy are not speaking to each other right now, but she talks about you all the time. When she starts talking about you, I be like, "Go mommy. You miss and love daddy, go ahead" (LOL). Alright, old man. I'm about to go get dressed so I can go to the mall with mommy and grandma. Grandma is buying me some Jordan 5's today. I got you and grandma wrapped around my finger (LOL). Be good, Daddy and come home soon. I love you so much.

Your Baby Girl,

Juel

MY VISION

Peace,
I was standing in the doorway of my cell.
You know, just doing the knowledge.
I had a beautiful vision.
We turned Shirley, this prison into a college and we all got knowledge.

Listen, listen many of us are sitting in prison for either trappin' or clappin'.
Now look at us, trapped IN these 8x10 cells.
The police yells, "Captain on the block."
The card games stop, we drop the rocks.

The chess players even get shook.
Whose move was it?
The Queen or the Rook?

Where did we learn such a horrible fear?
I got some books for you to read.
It's all in there.

I heard somebody the other day say, "Yo, you gotta fake it until you make it."
That hurt.
I got COMRADES that are going to die in prison and you talking about faking it?

What about your children?
I thought you told me you love your son?

Oh, I get it, prison's a game to you.
You having fun.

You know what's crazy about this whole situation?
We left our children in the world fatherless,
unprotected and we're in prison playing.

If your mother died tomorrow, how would you feel?
Well, my COMRADE, Shawn Jenkins, lost his
mother on Monday and on Friday the courts denied
his appeal.
Shawn Jenkins got a natural life sentence, THAT'S REAL!

I remember old man SMITTY told me to treat prison like its college.
He said study hard and get as much knowledge as you can.
He told me that in 2004, and at the time, he had 32 years in.
Another one of my COMRADES who's going to die in the pen.
How would our children look at us if they saw how we act in prison?

I had a beautiful vision.
We turned SHIRLEY, this prison into a college and we all got knowledge. But that was just a vision.
We are having fun in prison.
What about our children?

Peace,
Davon McNeil

MY PAIN RUNS DEEP

Look up at the sun. Look up at the moon. Look up at the stars... How beautiful they are. I would love to stand up here and give you fancy words, but I would be lying to you! I've spent the majority of my life standing on the curb...

So, can I tell you the truth right now?

I was 12 years old when I walked in on my mother...she had a needle stuck in her vein. Blood dripped down the center of her arm...etched on my mother's face was heavenly calm. She sat paralyzed within a dope fiend's nod...

Reflections: Ma? Ma? Mommy, what happened? Are you alright? Hi, baby. You hungry? How was school today? Go change your brother's diaper and you can go outside and play...

Traumatized! I never fully understood where my deep-rooted anger and intense self-hatred came from...I suffered from a severe case of apathy. No regard for another's pain...My emotions were eradicated! Feelings? I had none...

My heart grew icicled... frozen! It was numb...

Baby, please help me. Mommy is sick... C'mon Davon! Please help me. Mommy needs a fix... I would rather see you suffer before selling drugs to my mother!

My pain runs deep... So to be consoled I ran into the loving arms of Mrs. Streets. If you look within the cracks of the concrete, you'll find ancient scrolls of what my life use to be...

I was a hallway junkie...to escape my mother's addiction. I played the graveyard shift... My addiction was trappin', getting money and the feel of that plastic 5th on my hip....

My father abandoned me! He was trapped in the system... Mentally incarcerated. Physically in prison...

Blood in my eyez... Shootouts in broad day. Hoping a bullet hit me in the head so I can hurry and die... I wanted to die!

I use to pray to Allah...Lord, please come and get me and take me away... No more shooting... No more trappin'...no more pain...Satan's having his way.

Then a dark cloud formed and hovered over our block...most of us lost our lives confined to a cell. The rest got lined in chalk! Three-piece suits and hard bottoms...covered their bodies...stretched out in a box.

I watched my mother scratch her flesh until it turned raw and started to bleed...

Hi baby, you hungry? How was school today? Go change your brother's diaper and y'all go outside and play...

Peace,
Davon McNeil

MRS. STREETZ!

What if I told you that every once in a while, I shed a few tears?
My daughter's birthday was April 30th. She said, "Daddy, all I wanted was for you to be here."

It's been 13 years I ain't been there. It's my own fault that I'm here and couldn't be there.
So what if I shed a few tears. It hurts, man!

Didn't I share with y'all my truth about how my mother gets high by sticking needles in her veins? Damn man, you can't feel my pain?

I used to sit alone in my room thinking, "Damn, she loves that needle more than she loves me.
So I ran from home and went to hug Mrs. Streetz.

But Mrs. Streetz had no emotions and she wouldn't hug me back. Alright, you got that Mrs. Streetz, but I'll be back.
I'm gonna get even. I'm gonna sell everybody's mother crack! How you like that?

Mrs. Streetz laughed at me, right in my face. She said, "That's all you got? Here, take this case." Stop playing with me, that's just a taste.

Anger, frustration, hate started to set in. I'm plottin' now. I want revenge!
Mrs. Streetz must have been listening, because my

mom OD'd and Mrs. Streetz took out most of my friends.

She shot some with slugs, but she sent most to the pen,
She saved me for last and hit me with a life sentence!

What if I told you that every once in a while, I shed a few tears?

Peace,
Davon McNeil

I DON'T OWE THE STREETZ NOTHIN'!

Look at us! Spending our most precious years stuck in prison.
C'mon man, how are we truly livin'?

I come from that side street just like you. I spit crack in the palm of my hand and ran to cars just like you. I wore block uniforms just like you.

Champion hood with the point up under the leather;
Silver-tabbed Levi's with the Glock tucked in 'em.

If it wasn't Yums on my feet, I topped (tened) 'em!
I'm tellin' you, I was just like you...

Today you call it, turned up!
We simply called it, puttin' in work!

Oh, you a gangsta, you a thug and you squeeze the hammer?
Look at us now: duckin' out the chow hall, stealin' bananas.

Vee, you changed your life? You righteous now?
Word came back to the hood that you laid your stripes down.

The streets is talkin', Vee. They said you on some peace shit. They talkin' about you 5%!
You don't eat pork and you talkin' different! Vee,

what's good?

Let me tell you something! I don't owe the streets nothing! I stood on that corner all day and played that pissy hallway all night! I gave her everything. I gave the hood my life, literally!

I bled for the block! I bent that corner; let it go. Hot lead into flesh; broken bones. All for the love of the block! You know how much skin I lost, hittin' them fences runnin' from cops?

When them boys from the other side drove by and let them slugs fly, I caught one.

You ran on me! A year later you took the stand on me. I don't owe the hood nothin'!

"Daddy, when are you coming home? You've been in prison since I was a baby." She's 13. She'll be 14 on April 30th. She was just a baby. I watched her grow through pictures into a young lady.

The Streetz is talkin' about "I" changed my life! Damn right I changed my life!

The judge gave me life! I left my daughter and lost my wife! I don't owe the streets nothin'!

Did they tell you about my mother and how she's in the world struggling, battling chemical warfare, confined to a wheelchair? About my little brother who's facing the rest of his life here?

The streetz is talkin'! Yeah, I've made some

mistakes and fell victim to my lowest desires. Excommunicated and exiled feels like eternal fire.

B.U.T. through it all I built higher and higher.
Slowly I'm risen out of the fire!

I don't owe the streetz nothin'!

Please listen to my wisdom; it'll free you from your mental prison.
We can start building to destroy these physical prisons!

We're being used as tools. They're lying to our babies in public schools.
And then incarcerating them for being fooled...

I speak only the "truth," to show forth and prove my power!

Negative thinking brings forth negative livin'...

I was resurrected from a mental death by slashing the veil of ignorance!

I don't owe the streetz nothin'!

Peace,
Davon McNeil

BROKEN SPIRITS

How many of us would have broken spirits if our mothers died while we were sitting here in prison?

All alone in our cells trapped with mental visions of how fast and reckless we were living.

Would your spirit break if you were shackled in chains staring at your mother's beautiful face stiff in a casket at her wake?

Mother, please forgive me. I'm sorry... SHHH son, it's too late.

I told you so many times to change your ways of living. Now I've died, and you will never see me again. Son, I prayed, and I prayed, but you got caught up in your sins.

Your spirit is slowly breaking; your own life, contemplating should you take it?

Your mother was all you had. Like me, you never knew your dad.

Alone in your cell you hear her soft and sweet voice: My dear son, do not be like your father. Be there for your daughters.

Your father left us while you were growing within my womb.

Son, please come visit me when you're released from prison and leave pretty flowers on my tomb.

Look at those four concrete walls that have you physically boxed in a cell. Get up off your knees praying to be with me in heaven.

Son, you're in hell!

Heaven is where you create it...

My son, our spirits are one now. Pure energy. Don't let them divine evils break it!

Baby, Satan is a liar! Prison is the fire!

Create heaven right there, right now. There is nothing above the sky and there is nothing below the ground...

My son, can you see me now?
Look up into the heavens.
Within your mental I'm smiling down...

Do not allow your spirit to be broken!

Peace,
Davon McNeil

DAVON, PLEASE UNDERSTAND

After 12 years of being strong and struggling to hold on, my wife decided it was time to let go and move on with her life.

She did her best to explain why she had to walk away.
She said, Davon please try to understand.
I want a real life.
What we are doing is not genuine.
It is based on fantasy.

I want to be held.
I want to be touched.
I want to be wrapped within your arms at night when I fall asleep.
I gave you all that I had to give and my all was not enough.
Davon, we didn't leave you, you left us!

When you were hungry, I kept you well-fed.
After you got shot and came home from the hospital, I cleaned your wounds when they bled.
Davon, I even stayed after I caught you with that bitch in my bed.

Please don't hate me.
But if I don't leave now, I'm going to go crazy.
My life revolves around prison visits, collect calls and mail.

Davon, have you considered how my heart feels?

You told me you were coming home on your last appeal.
You said time served would be the deal and you would make all of our dreams become real.

Davon, I swear this is not about another man.
I don't want this life for Juel.
She's starting to understand.

Mommy, why do we have to go see daddy in that faraway place?
Mommy, is that daddy's home?
Mommy who's that person that interrupts when I'm talking to daddy on the phone?

I stayed with you for 21 years.
So many tears, so many fears, so many nights you weren't there.
Davon, out of 21 years, you've only spent 6 physically here.

It's always been about you.
What about me!
Davon, I have needs.

I love you so much and you taught me what it means to be at peace. I gave you all of me and you gave all of yourself to the streetz.

Davon, please try to understand.

To accept this call, please press 0.

Hello?
Who's this?
Jason!
Damn (smile)...

Peace,
Davon McNeil

PEACE AND BLESSINGS

There was a time in my life where "I" couldn't find my own way out of the triple stages of darkness.

I was a young black man and the street corner was my sandbox. I stood still and all of my thoughts were completely empty.

My mother was fighting the battle of addiction. My father was situated within a physical prison.

While most young children were playing hide-and-seek, I was a young child lost in them cold streets.

I was filled up with self-hatred and violent anger. They stole my history and had me surrounded by strangers.

As I continued my journey down your yellow brick road, I never found the promised pot of gold.

But I did stumble into a place where most faces look just like mine and we share a similar story of a lost history, fed falsehoods of a Divine Mystery.

Today I realize that my life does matter, and I can climb as high as I desire, as long as I remain focused on each step of the success ladder!

Peace,
Davon McNeil

WE CAME TO SEE YOU, BUT WE COULDN'T GET IN...

Hey... I bet you're mad and under the assumption that we didn't come out to see you on Saturday, but we did. We actually wasted an entire Saturday for nothing. We drove all the way out there: an hour and fifteen minutes. We waited in the waiting room: an hour and a half. We went to go in and they informed me that my jeans were too tight and I needed to leave and go to Target to buy new pants. I was pissed. I had a plumber at my house that I had to pay, and I had already put gas in my car and money on the card. So the last thing I wanted to do was pay for new pants because I was broke.

After I calmed down, I went to Target and bought corduroys which were so loose I needed a belt. I went back. I filled out my paperwork again only for the next lady to tell me the new pants were too tight. Really! So, I left. I had to drive all the way home, another hour and fifteen minutes wasted.

So, we did come; we did everything we could; and I wasted a lot of money that I didn't have for nothing. And as mad as you were about thinking we didn't show up, imagine how mad I was about wasting money on a card, wasting a half tank of gas at $3.48 a gallon, wasting money on pants I will never wear again and never mind wasting an entire five and a half hours of a Saturday where I could have been getting things done. So, I'm sorry we didn't get in to see you but believe me, we tried like hell!

XOXO
Melanie

IT WAS COLD OUT THERE

I left home as a young boy, searching for myself and my share of gold. Unaware that them streets were going to be icy cold.
I've spent long days and even longer nights.
In piss-stained hallways selling drugs and shooting dice.

It was cold out there.

Champion hoods under leather coats,
Finely creased silver tab jeans.
And top ten Adidas were uniforms I wore.
I've spent infinite hours spiting crack in front of Store 24.

It was cold out there.

I gave 'em 3 for 50, 6 for 100, maybe 7 if I was blunted.
Damn, I miss them rush hours, them shits were the best.
C'mon, tell me the truth, what do you know about late nights in the hood, Ducking the D's, Glock on the waistline, and vest on the chest?

It was cold out there.

I had to measure each step that I took,
while in them streets hustling, grinding, surrounded by killers and crooks. I lost many of my comrades

to hollow tip slugs.
For me, it was way more than shooting guns and selling drugs.

It was the lifestyle, I did it for love.
Now look at me, sitting in prison.

It was cold out there...

Born from the mind of Davon McNeil

MY FIRST BORN CHILD

To my first-born child.
It was you who made me a father (smile).

I was 15 ½ and now I have a daughter. What did I know about being a father? Your grandmother is my mother as well as my father.

I cut your umbilical cord and I almost passed out (smile).
When the doctor slapped your behind, I wanted to punch him out... (seriously).

I looked you in your dark eyes and I said, I love you baby.
One day you're going to be a grown woman, but you'll always be daddy's baby.

It seems as though you've grown up so fast. 21 years have passed and now you're such a beautiful little lady. I still see you inside your playpen. It seems like just yesterday you were a baby.

Shalese, you don't know this, but at times I cry in this cell.
If I knew then what I know now, I would have done my duty as a father very well.

I'm so glad you understand and love your father because you're the reason that I go harder at getting home to my baby. My first born. My daughter.

Today you're a beautiful little lady but remember this: you'll always be daddy's baby!

I love you, Shalese
Daddy

PAIN IN MY HEART

I got pain in my heart because the streets touched my brothers.
I called collect to my mother and through hot tears she said,
"Davon, they shot your brother."

I got pain in my heart because the streets touched my brothers...

I put this on all that I love and hold dear to my heart.
It was Fox 25 which told me my little brother got knocked...
They said, "Cold case solved;
Brockton man arrested!"

Homicide, FBI and the DEA raided the spot.
They found him in a crawl space hiding in the attic.
The paper said he was vested and close by they found a semi-automatic.

I got pain in my heart, so by no means am I glorifying the negative lifestyle I come from. But I'd be lying to you if I said that my past life wasn't lived by the gun!

I got pain in my heart knowing I sold poison to single mothers...

Now that I knowledge (know) the truth, I can't

promise you that I'll recover.
Come walk with me on a hot summer day.
We're going to take a stroll through the cemetery!
I got brothers there.

I got pain in my heart because the streets touched my mother...

Let me ask you a question?
When are we going to start appreciating our mothers?

My momma, she don't got no legs!
She lost 'em when I was in Shirley Max!
I couldn't see the realness.
I was still mentally dead!
The nurse's pin was still stuck in my head.

I got pain in my heart, but I got the knowledge now...

Life still hard!
Just look around.
I see so many original faces locked in the system.
Wake up!
Afeni Shakur almost lost her life and Tupac's while trapped in prison.

I got pain in my heart, but I'm going to cut my wisdom...

When we're locked in that cell, let's all pick up a book!
Learn who you truly are.

Then you'll fully understand why you're trapped behind bars!
All praise (Be) to the Father (Allah)!

Peace,
Davon McNeil

CHOICES

People advocate poor choices and as a result oftentimes they find themselves existing within a prison or penitentiary complex because of it. There is nothing funny or entertaining about prison; from the cold steel which surrounds and engulfs you to the repetitive food consumption. It's not a guarantee that you will make it out either. In fact, when you first enter into prison you go to what is called "Intake" (commonly known as Process of Intake). One of the first questions the guard asks you is, "Where do you want your body to be sent should you become deceased?" That question alone not only shocked I-SUN b.u.t. I realized from that point on I would not only have to fight, b.u.t. fight and secure my freedom (light) in order to escape this madness in which I now reside. Somehow, I was fortunate enough to have an out date, meaning I would need to serve a ten-year (10) prison sentence before I would see the light (home) again.

Prison can become one of the loneliest and depressing experiences, especially for the individual who wishes to succeed or for the individual who is nearing their release date with the determination to never return to prison again. Unfortunately, there are those brothers who have come to terms with the idea that this place (prison) is where they will forever reside until death snatches them from this reality. I've met brothers who have come to the realization that they will never be physically free again, all because of a poor choice they regretfully made 10, 20 or 30 years ago.

In life, every action is derived from a choice. Of course, there is a process to decision-making, or at least there should be. We should not just make rash decisions. We should meditate on them, analyze them, categorize them and then proceed. Taking the steps just mentioned is known as informed decision-making; decisions made based upon the knowledge we momentarily obtain at that time within our universal mind. It's easier said than done b.u.t. the process must be completed before we make any decisions, or we will live to regret it later. Choices!

CAREFULLY HEED OPTIONS INCLUDING CONSTRUCTIVE ELEMENTS SUCCESSFULLY

Peace!
Allah Manifest!
D. Golston

I REMEMBER

PEACE TO THE GOD, VEE!

Well, you already know we go back to them Reservoir street days when you had that green two-door Honda hatchback. You took me on my very first blunt ride (although I didn't smoke, I still caught a contact). During that ride I met a lot of "Hood Legends." Nature took its course and led us down a path which our mothers never wanted for us "Fam." Now prison has transformed us for the better life that's ahead. You blessed me by letting me read your book and its "jewels" all throughout, so I had to hit the archives to bless you right back.

MEANING

Meaning is not something you can stumble across like the answer to a riddle or the prize in a treasure hunt. Meaning is something you build into your life. You build it out of your own past, out of your affections and loyalties, out of experience of humankind as it is passed on to you, out of your own talent and understanding, out of the values for which you are willing to sacrifice something. The ingredients are there. You are the only one who can put them together into a pattern which will be your life. Let it be a life which has dignity and meaning you stand for. If it does then the particular balance of success or failure is of less account.

One Love, One Life!
Your Comrade 4-Life,
Boogieman

IT'S NOT A GAME AT ALL

Truth Power (2016)
Master.Allah.Why (May)
Wisdom Knowledge (21)

I used the Drug Game and its relevant conduct as a stage to say, "Look at me."

The so-called "Drug Game" is not a game at all. A game is an activity which provides entertainment or amusement. In any game you do one of two things: win or lose. This Drug Game takes no prisoners; it plays for keeps. Lives are lost, families are destroyed and there's no winning. We overlooked the losses because we made our money, had our women and we savagely pursued whatever it was that we thought made us happy at any given time.

This is the process of addiction. We did not see our losses; we somehow thought we were winning. However, as we continue to live these self-destructive and socially destructive ways of life we are losing ourselves, forfeiting our goals and dreams for the pursuit of instant gratifications which only mask our true issues.

I am no longer in mind, character or culture to commit crime on any level. "The Streets Lied and I Believed."

A therapeutic manifestation of Truth from a Brother

in God who is constantly in the labor of the Righteous.

P.ositive E.nergy A.ctivates C.onstant E.levation (Peace)

Righteous: Truth Magnetic Allah
Honorable: Jermain M. Hunter

CONCLUSION

My best work of art has been my own life which I forge and live out according to my own creative will. By learning to resist my lower self—which manifest learned destructive habits—I was able to construct a realm of positive desires. Ten years ago, I made the conscious choice to change my life for the better by utilizing my time in prison to transcend my criminal- addictive thinking and behavior; thus, becoming the best person I can be. My transition from negative to positive has not been an easy task, but it's been well worth it.

I've come to the divine realization that to change my reality (life), a prerequisite was that I change my mentality (way of thinking). Prior to incarceration, my life was founded upon ignorance and lies. My pliable young mind was conditioned to believe that criminality was a culture which I would excel within. Therefore, selling drugs; carrying guns; living each day with reckless abandon; and not fearing tomorrow was the order of the day for me.

Today, my life has meaning and purpose. I've dedicated my life to the cause of enlightening our youths. Young people are being lied to and led astray by a wicked force (the streets). They are being socially engineered and mentally manipulated to believe that living a life of crime and coming to prison is a badge of honor. Therefore, I've taken on the duty and responsibility of crushing those myths, just as I accepted responsibility for

taking a young man's life as a direct result of adhering to those ominous and destructive myths.

I will never be able to fully verbally express the experience of living my life confined to an 8'xlO' cold and lonely casket (prison cell). I've endured and witnessed some of the most atrocious, barbaric, uncivilized, beastly, mind-breaking, soul-shattering, inhumane and traumatic acts while being trapped within "the belly of the beast" aka prison. I've met thousands of men who suppressed their emotions as children to be able to traverse the harsh realities of the world into which they were born Some of us are truly great men who made serious mistakes in our young lives. However, it does not change the fact that our mistakes shattered innocent families and caused tremendous pain towards others.

I want to share with youths my experiences while spending the past sixteen years of my life in prison. I want to share with them the tremendous pain I endured when my mother passed away. She never had the opportunity to witness my transformation from negative to positive. I want to tell them about my so-called friends who have long forgotten about me; about my experiences while living in an 8'xlO' prison cell with men who have been sentenced to spend the remainder of their natural lives in prison;

about leaving my two beautiful daughters alone out there in this cold world without the guidance and protection of their father. I simply want to tell them the TRUTH!

Please help me in this urgent mission by spreading the word about my book: *The Streets Lied and We Believed*. This book was created by me and other incarcerated men whose objective is to awaken the youth of today from their deep sleep (ignorance). I can be of service and value to them if given a chance! Thank you.

ABOUT THE AUTHOR

My name is Davon McNeil and I was born in Boston, Massachusetts. Growing up, my mother was a single parent because my father spent the majority of my life incarcerated. At a very young age I was exposed to a way of life which many people call "the game." The very people who were responsible for my upbringing and wellbeing are the same ones who would stuff my diaper as an infant with balloons filled with an assortment of drugs—marijuana, pills, cocaine, heroin, etc.—and sneak them into various prisons for my father, who used the money he made from selling these drugs to survive.

At 12 years of age, when most kids my age were riding their bicycle or playing video games, I was on the street corner selling crack cocaine and carrying guns. And on September 15, 2003, I was tried and convicted of second-degree murder and sentenced to second-degree life which means I will go before a parole board after serving 15 years of my life in prison. But instead of becoming angry and bitter, I utilized my time to become a better person instead of a better criminal. I made a conscious choice to change my life for the better.

I'm proud to admit that during the 16 years I've served I have avoided being a part of any physical altercations with another inmate or officer. I spend 100% of my time becoming a better man. And I am committed to spending the rest of my days on earth dedicated to bringing awareness to youth and being of service to others. Peace!

Made in the USA
Middletown, DE
19 July 2022